Guide to Fishing

WEST CANADA CREEK

AND ITS
TRIBUTARIES

By M. Paul Keesler

Photos by the author unless otherwise noted
Maps drawn by Gary Williams

Cover Photo Location: Fishing Rock near Middleville

GUIDE TO FISHING
WEST CANADA CREEK AND ITS TRIBUTARIES
By M. Paul Keesler

Copyright 1997

Photographs by the author unless otherwise noted
Maps drawn by Gary Williams

**LIBRARY OF CONGRESS
CATALOG CARD NUMBER 97-093375**

Keesler, M. Paul
Prospect, New York
Mid-York Sportsman, Inc.
Prospect, New York

ISBN 0-9645372-2-2

Price $12.95 US

**North Country Books
Distributor
311 Turner Street—Box 217, Utica, NY 13501-1727**

Dedicated to the memory of
Leo "Jack" McDiarmid

WEST CANADA CREEK

She starts as a trickle in the Adirondack wilderness. Nourished by ancient ponds, lakes and mountain streams, she grows slowly, meanders through wooded valleys, plummets down granite precipices, gushes through a glacier-sculptured gorge . . . and meets civilization at Hinckley Lake.

Her wildness is tamed by Hinckley dam and downstream power dams, but she continues to carve the limestone of Trenton Gorge and offers springtime spectacle as she descends Prospect Falls and the remaining cascades of Trenton Falls. When she exits the gorge at the village of Trenton Falls she is wild again. Her waters rush and riffle as she courses down her valley, past the villages of Poland, Newport and Middleville, on to Herkimer where her mountain waters merge with the Mohawk River.

She is West Canada Creek, one of New York's premier trout waters.

CONTENTS

ACKNOWLEDGMENTS

Jane Dieffenbacher (historian) for sharing the unpublished *"Reminiscences of Sherman O. Klock"*, an invaluable source of information about fish and fishing in West Canada Valley in the late 1800s and early 1900s.

Jack Hasse (fisheries biologist) for providing a wealth of historical information on the management of this fishery; for spending hours answering questions, reviewing maps, correcting mistakes and misconceptions, and finally, for so successfully managing the West Canada fishery for more than 20 years.

Muriel Fenner and **Margery Foss** (historians) for sharing *"William S. Benchley's Journal" (1850s–1860s)*The Trume Haskell Family for allowing me to read their camp "Guest Books" (1941–1995). **Richard Preall** (fisheries biologist) for providing information on the upper valley fishery.

Steve Burton for allowing me to photograph the entire valley from his helicopter.

Jack McDiarmid for introducing me to the "real" West Canada Creek and for sharing his knowledge and experiences fly fishing "West Creek". **John Bianco** for sharing his knowledge of fly fishing West Canada Creek and showing me how to catch my first West Canada trout on a fly. **Randy Kulig** for allowing me to tap into his reservoir of information on fly tying, fly fishing and the West Canada Creek fishery. **Bill Shumway** and **Ron Gugnacki** for sharing their knowledge and experiences fishing the tributaries.

John Pratt for sharing his photo of Hinckley in the 1920s and **James Klosek** for the photo of his trophy taken in 1995.

West Canada Creek landowners for sharing their backyards with fishermen. Mohawk Valley Chapter Trout Unlimited, Herkimer County Conservation Alliance, Federated Sportsmen Clubs of Oneida County and the New York State Department of Environmental Conservation for their continuing efforts to provide quality fishing on West Canada Creek, including stocking fish, monitoring water flow and water quality, and supporting fishery management programs that provide quality fishing for all.

John Pitarresi for reading the manuscript, offering suggestions and writing the Forward.

And finally, my wife **Gert** for her patience and good humor, and for reading every chapter many times over to find misspelled words and lost punctuation.

FORWARD

Everyone knows West Canada Creek.

You look at the map and see that long blue line jaggedly snaking its way out of the Adirondacks and down into the heart of the Mohawk Valley.

Big Water. Good trout stream. One of the best.

All true, but who really knows the West Canada—its lore, its natural history, its suffering at the hands of man, how to make use of its recreational bounty, the prospects for its future?

Paul Keesler does, and in this book he shares that knowledge with us.

Paul has fished the West Canada for more than 35 years and has lived within casting distance of the creek for most of that time, but he wasn't satisfied simply with his own experience. He dug into the history of the West Canada, consulted old journals and reports, walked and talked and explored with both old-timers and younger outdoor adventurers who know the water well, picked the brains of fisheries biologists and even took flight to gain a unique perspective of his subject.

The result is doubly satisfying—a very interesting picture of one of New York State's prime recreational resources and an extremely useful guide to how to best take advantage of it.

You will enjoy this book, and you will find it useful, too. You can't do much better than that.

John Pitarresi
Outdoor Columnist
Utica Observer Dispatch

INTRODUCTION

This book started as a chapter for a book on West Canada Valley that I plan to publish in 1998, however, my "research" produced so much information about fish and fishing in this area, I couldn't wait to share it.

Although I've fished West Canada Creek for more than 35 years, and have written about it in several magazine articles and in a book on canoe-fishing, I had no idea how much fascinating information I'd discover in old newspapers, diaries, unpublished manuscripts and biological reports. Nor did I realize how little I knew about West Canada fish and fishing until I talked to some expert fishermen and fisheries biologists.

My research for the "Big Book" on West Canada Valley included a 10-mile backpacking trip into the West Canada Lakes Wilderness Area where the West Canada is born, so early on I developed a better understanding of this remote region and its past and present fishing opportunities.

This research also included hikes up or canoe trips down the major tributaries in the valley below Trenton Falls and a few streams in the upper valley. On all of these trips I carried cameras, notebook .... and an ultralight spinning rod. In addition to noting the vegetation, wildlife, waterfalls, old mill sites and bridges, I discovered brown trout, brook trout and fallfish.

And to get a better understanding of the entire watershed that feeds this 76-mile long river— no one could possibly fish it all— I photographed it from a helicopter.

From all of this information, I've selected enough history, where, what and how-to information, plus illustrations, photographs and maps to make this book useful to anyone who fishes the river and its tributaries.

While the history of this fishery is fascinating to me and a few other fishing fanatics who believe the only way to appreciate the present is to understand the past, it's not necessary to know it to catch fish. So, if history is not your thing, just skip to the where, what and how-to chapters. I'd be remiss if I didn't point out that this history includes some clues to the location of some little-known wild trout fishing.

 Experienced fishermen need to know what kind of fish are in the river and tributaries, how to get to the best areas to fish. Novice spin and, fly fishermen need that same information, plus some basic instructions on how to catch fish. All of the above and much more are included.

Perhaps the most important part of this book is the map section. It provides more information about access to this fishery than has ever been published. The map section is divided into two parts.

The lower river and its tributaries, from Trenton Falls to Herkimer, are by far the most productive fishery, so more detailed maps are provided.

The upper river and the south branch offers some productive stretches of trout water, but they are generally near stream and lake outlets, so less detailed maps are provided. The upper river section also includes the source-lakes, other watershed lakes, plus Hinckley Lake and Prospect Pond.

There is also a chapter on float-fishing, plus information on sport shops, guide services, campsites, cabins, restaurants and valley attractions. If I missed something important, let me know so I can include it in the Big Book on West Canada Valley.

                                        M. Paul Keesler

Chapter 1

WHAT'S IN A NAME?

RIVER NOT A CREEK

Calling the West Canada a "creek" is like calling Arnold Schwarzenegger a wimp. It's 76 miles long and dumps more water into the Mohawk River than any other stream. With a watershed of 569 square miles and a water flow as high as 1337 cubic feet per second, it's a much larger stream than many of the rivers in New York State.

Webster's Dictionary considers a *creek as*, "a small stream, especially a shallow or intermittent tributary to a river." The West Canada certainly doesn't fit that description. So, why "creek" and not "river"?

John Sherman, the "father" of Trenton Falls, refers to the West Canada as "the river" in his essays published in the 1851 book, *Trenton Falls—Illustrated*. The editor of that book likened the West Canada flowing into the Mohawk to the Missouri flowing into the Mississippi.

Charles A. Gianni in a feature article on the West Canada Valley in the January 29, 1928 *Utica Observer Dispatch* noted:

"Why this stream, 75 or more miles in length and of good width, was originally called a creek has always been a source of wonder to me. I have seen many so called rivers in both the East and West that could be drowned in its waters."

In his 1946 book, *"West Canada Creek,"* author David H. Beetle, notes" . . . the West Canada is a good river to know," and refers to it as "the river" throughout his book.

When I began the research for a book on West Canada Valley, my first task was to discover why this river was called a creek. I didn't realize how long the path to discovery would be or how many names this river has had over the years.

The path of my research will be discussed in depth in the book **KUYAHOORA—DISCOVERING WEST CANADA VALLEY,** however, the results of what I learned after months of studying old maps, documents and books are offered here.

The Mohawk Indians called the river **Deyoghtoraron or Te-ugh'-ta-ra'-row** which referred to "colored waters."

Kanata is another Indian word for the river that some references indicated meant colored water, more specifically "amber waters." Kanata and Canada sound so much alike, I wondered if they were the same word. Recent Information provided by the Oneida Indian Nation notes the literal translation of "kanata" is "village," and that it is the origin of the word "Canada". There was an ancient, pre-Iroquois League, settlement at the mouth of the river.

The Falls was called **Kuyahoora**, meaning "leaping waters," and the river was called by that name.

The Senecas called the river **Te-uge'-ga** and considered it the source of the Mohawk River.

The first Europeans to settle and travel extensively in the area were Dutch. Using the Indian word Canada (or perhaps Kanata) they called the river **Canada Kill.** Kill is the Dutch word for stream, i.e., Batten Kill, Lansing Kill, Keyser Kill, etc. The English living in the area called it Canada Kill or **Canada Creek**. At least one 18th century surveyor recognized the size of this stream and called it **Canada River.**

For a time the western boundary of the Royal Grant (66,000 acres of land purchased by Sir William Johnson from the Mohawk Indians in the mid 1700s) was called either Canada River or Canada Creek, and the eastern boundary was called Canada Creek or Lower Canada Creek. Around 1800, the names of *all* the streams that flowed into the Mohawk were designated Creeks, regardless of their size. At that time, the Royal Grant boundary streams were named East Canada Creek and **West Canada Creek.**

Since that time there have been a number of attempts to change the name of the river, the valley and Hinckley Lake to **Kuyahoora**. While none of them were successful, this Indian name lives on in the communities along the river. There are for instance, Kuyahoora Valley Historical Society, Kuyahoora Volunteer Ambulance Corporation, Kuyahoora Inn, Kuyahoora Outdoor Center, Kuyahoora Valley Park and Kuyahoora Valley Rangers.

Whatever the name, make no mistake, the West Canada is a river not a creek.

OLD NAMES, NEW NAMES, NO NAMES

TRIBUTARY STREAMS

Many of the tributary streams have had more than one name over the years; some of them have no published names. Even recent maps of different origin indicate different names for the streams. Wherever possible I have included both names. In the case of the no-name streams, I created a name from a nearby landmark or historical site.

POOLS, RUNS AND RIFFS

Some of the most popular fishing pools, runs and riffs have long established names, however, many of them don't have names, other than what each fisherman calls his favorite stretch of river. After interviewing a number of West Canada anglers, I used long-established names, like "Stedson's Run" and "Blue Barn Bend"; consensus names like "The Lake" and "The Canyon"; names created from landmarks or lay of the land like "Boulder Run" and "High Banks", and finally, the names of fishermen who have enjoyed years of fishing particular stretches of the river, and who contributed significantly to the West Canada fishery.

    If I have misnamed any of the tributaries or fish havens, or you have suggestions for other names, please let me know.

Chapter 2

200 YEARS
UP AND DOWN FISHERY

Today West Canada Creek **below** Trenton Falls is one of New York's premier brown trout streams. A hundred years ago there were no trout in this area of the stream. Two hundred years ago this was brook trout water. The history of this up and down fishery is interesting, enlightening and encouraging.

The West Canada **above** Trenton Falls was a famous New York trout fishery when the downstream fishery was nonexistent, and remained so well into the mid 1900's. This history of this once renowned fishery is interesting, depressing and discouraging—with a few rays of hope.

NO SHAD, NO STRIPERS

The West Canada was never a major fishery. Spawning shad and striped bass that came up the Hudson River couldn't get over the falls at Cohoes, so they never got into the Mohawk River and up the West Canada.

Brook trout, bass, fallfish, and suckers inhabited this river below the big falls. During the *spring* when suckers, fallfish and bass spawned, and in the *fall* when brook trout spawned, there were concentrations of these fish in many areas. Indians and early settlers could spear, net and angle for these spawning fish with great success at the mouth of the river, below rapids and falls and in tributary streams. (There were no bass or fallfish above Trenton Falls)

During the summer months when the water level went down and the water temperature went up, most of the West Canada was very poor habitat for trout. Brook trout survived below falls, in the deepest pools, and where springs and spring-fed tributary streams provided cold water year round. Suckers, fallfish and bass fared better, but their habitat was also limited.

WEST CANADA CREEK
AND
ITS TRIBUTARIES

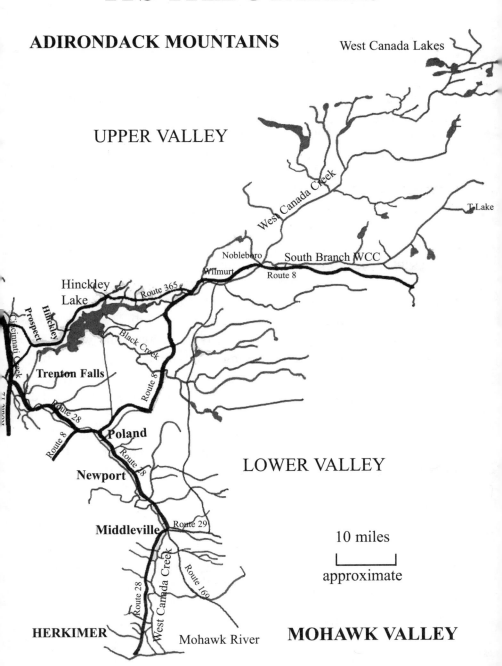

ADIRONDACK MOUNTAINS

West Canada Lakes

UPPER VALLEY

West Canada Creek

T-Lake

Nobleboro

South Branch WCC

Wilmurt

Route 8

Hinckley
Lake

Route 365

Cincinnati Creek

Prospect

Hinckley

Black Creek

Route 8

Trenton Falls

Route 8

Route 28

Route 8

Poland

Route 8

Newport

LOWER VALLEY

Middleville

Route 29

10 miles

approximate

West Canada Creek

Route 169

Route 28

HERKIMER

West Canada Creek

Mohawk River

MOHAWK VALLEY

TRIBUTARIES HURT, RIVER SPARED

When this area was opened for settlement around 1790 there was neither the financial resources or technologies available to build mill dams on the main stream. (Early attempts were destroyed by spring runoffs.) However, the valley's many tributaries, where there were numerous waterfalls—and where mill dams were not so easily washed away—were much easier to manage. These smaller streams provided the waterpower to run the first sawmills and gristmills, and became the sites for tanneries, distilleries and fabric processing mills.

While this use of water and subsequent pollution, especially during the summer months, dramatically affected the fish populations in tributary streams, the West Canada itself still provided excellent brook trout fishing where the water was cold enough and deep enough.

A TRICKLE OF WATER BETWEEN MILL DAMS

Around 1800 mill dams were constructed on the West Canada at Newport and at Trenton Falls, and by 1825 there were additional mill dams at the villages of Middleville, Trenton Falls, Prospect and near the present village of Hinckley. During low water periods, these mill dams dramatically restricted the flow of water. The result was that during those critical summer months, the West Canada and many of its tributaries became trickles of water between mill dams.

At first this trickle of water was polluted with the wastes of gristmills, sawmills, wool processing and dying mills, asheries, distilleries and tanneries. In the mid 1800s the pollutants from cheese factories were added to tributary streams and to the river. At times the river ran milky white, yellow, green, brown or red.

By the 1840s the only fish caught were fallfish, chubs and a few bullheads that survived near the mill dams and some of the deeper holes in the river. Except at the mouths of a few tributary streams, brook trout and bass were practically nonexistent in the river below Trenton Falls.

TRIBUTARIES ON THE MEND

While stream conditions deteriorated in the river, they improved in some of the tributary streams. Most of the forests were cleared from the valley and planted to wheat, rye, corn and potatoes, or to provide hay and pasture for sheep, horses and cattle. Groundwater that was

Sulfides from the Hinckley pulp mills polluted the lower river even after the dam was built. (photo courtesy of John Pratt)

previously sucked up by a vast forest of hardwoods, was now available to raise the water table and provide more cold water for valley-side streams. And, as the output of the big mills on the river increased, many of the small-stream mills closed down, improving tributary fishing even more. Streams such as Black Creek, Wolf Hollow, Hurricane and Cold Brook consistently produced baskets of brook trout up to one pound.

THE WORST AND BEST STARTED AT HINCKLEY

Around 1840 a large sawmill using "ganged" circular saws was built on the river at Gang Mills (Hinckley). Here began a series of events that accelerated the 100-year decimation of the downstream fishery . . . and set the stage for creating one of the finest brown trout streams in the state.

As the forests of large softwood trees that fed "Gang Mills" were depleted, a new industry developed at Hinckley around 1880. Millions of smaller softwoods covered upstream mountains and valleys. This "pulpwood" was floated down the West Canada to Gang Mills where it was barked, chopped up and "cooked" in huge vats of sulfuric acid. The resulting pulp was used to make paper and rayon. The resulting sulfide pollution doomed the downstream trout fishery for another 45 years.

FAMOUS FISH HAVENS GONE FOREVER

Upstream from Gang Mills two, three and sometimes 4-pound brook trout were taken from deep holes and runs on worms and flies.

Two of the most productive areas were the deep hole at "The Forks" where Black Creek entered the West Canada, and at "Hess's Rift," just upstream from the streamside village of Northwood. Both of these legendary fish havens (and the village) are now under the waters of Hinckley Lake.

HINCKLEY LAKE SETS THE STAGE FOR DOWNSTREAM FISHERY

Hinckley Lake was created in 1915 to provide a continuous supply of water for the Barge Canal and to control downstream flooding. The potential for a downstream fishery grew with leaps and bounds with the construction of Hinckley Dam, although it wasn't realized for many years. For a few years this new lake produced some exceptional catches of brook trout. Stringers of 2-pounders taken from the lake and its tributaries were quite common.

Lowering the lake level during the winter in preparation for the Spring runoff and the subsequent high-water flooding of the lake, eventually flushed nutrient-rich farm-soils downstream, leaving a lake-bottom of sand, gravel and rock. The mountain river and tributaries feeding the lake were (and still are) so low in nutrients that the number and size of fish declined in the reservoir.

NO FISH FOR THE WEST CANADA UNTIL 1924

Although both the state and federal government were stocking fish in area streams in the 1890s, no fish were stocked in the West Canada because of the sulfide pollution from the Hinckley pulp mill. The mill ceased operation around 1922 and the first trout were stocked in the West Canada in 1924. They came from the Federal Hatchery at Barneveld.

UPSTREAM - BROOK TROUT REIGNED SUPREME

Upstream from Hinckley Lake all the way to the source of the river at West Canada Lakes, brook trout reigned supreme. At first this Adirondack Mountain river and its tributaries were protected by their remoteness. The soil was poor and winters long, so the earliest attempts at farming failed. No farms, no people, no roads.

Even after the forests were logged over and logs and silt filled mountain streams, brook trout survived in unaffected areas and moved back to the ravaged areas when they recovered. Logging operations temporarily improved trout habitat in some areas by creating impoundments and by releasing nutrient rich soil (thin as it was) into the watershed.

Anglers who fished this area measured their catches in pounds of fish caught. Well into the 1900s taking 30–50 pounds of brook trout from stillwaters, big holes, near stream and lake outlets, and in ponds and lakes was quite common. Most of these fish weighed less than a pound, but some waters held two and even three-pounders.

MOUNTAIN FISHERY DECLINES

This mountain fishery declined throughout the 1900s partly due to increased access provided by lumbering roads and float planes, and partly due to the effects of acid precipitation. This 20th Century phenomenon of increased concentrations of sulfides and nitrates in the air, from smokestacks as far west as Indiana, created acid-laden rain and snowfall that raised the acid level in some Adirondack waters so high nothing could live in them. While most West Canada waters were spared such devastation, an increase in acidity in the areas of granite rock and thin soils, affected the brook trout's food supply and caused a decline in size and numbers.

WEST CANADA GETS ITS SHARE OF STOCKED FISH

Soon after the sulfide pollution ended at Hinckley, a fish-stocking program started in West Canada waters, including Hinckley Lake. These fish came from both state and federal hatcheries.

From 1924 to 1933 the West Canada and it's tributaries received: 198,725 brown trout; 111,485 speckled (brook) trout; 24,875 rainbow trout. Most of the trout stocked were 3-inch fry. In addition to trout, warmwater species were also stocked in the West Canada and included: 9,800 smallmouth bass; 11,000 yellow perch; 500,000 pike-perch (walleye fry), and 28 bullheads. .

Hinckley Lake received: 5,900 lake trout; 10,500 rainbow trout, and 61,000 speckled (brook) trout. Smaller ponds and impoundments in the West Canada watershed received 26,350 lake trout; 102,175 speckled (brook) trout; 2,850 rainbow trout, and 30 bullheads. Again mostly 3-inch fry were stocked.

1934 BIOLOGICAL SURVEY
STUDIES THE WEST CANADA

A 1934 Biological Survey by the New York State Conservation Department evaluated the success of this stocking program, provided observations and recommended changes.

The report begins with the following observation about the West Canada:

"It includes much good trout water, but contrary to usual expectation summer conditions in the upper part of the stream are less favorable for trout than those in the several miles below Hinckley Dam."

A description in this report of the West Canada below Hinckley sheds some light on the condition of the stream at the time and helps to understand the recommended stocking of fish in this area.

"The creek leaves Hinckley Reservoir clear, clean and cold enough for trout. It receives a slight amount of pollution from the village of Hinckley and slightly more from Prospect, two miles downstream. From Hinckley to Prospect the stream flows swiftly over a bed studded with large glacial boulders. At Prospect, the creek turns to flow through two miles of deep gorge to Trenton Falls. Here during times of low water, from 50 to 180 cubic feet per second of water is diverted into a feeder for the Barge Canal. The low rate of flow of West Canada Creek at this point is about 375 cubic feet per second.

"Passing the canal feeder, the water flows swiftly over a short stretch of bouldery bottom, receives pollution from Trenton Falls (the village), and starts a ten-mile stretch of quiet water interrupted only by short riffles. Poland adds its pollution to the creek near the lower end of this stretch. The region of quiet water ends at a belt of Little Falls Dolomite bedrock about a mile below Poland. Large glacial boulders are absent in this quiet water region, but are characteristic of the creek bed from below Poland almost to Herkimer. From Poland to near its mouth, the creek is uniformly broad, shallow, rocky and swift.

"Four miles below Poland , Newport adds its sewage and six miles farther downstream, Middleville, with its tannery wastes and sewage, adds the most serious pollution encountered during the entire course of the stream. About two miles below Middleville the

Herkimer County Home, pours raw sewage into the nearby creek.

"A dam about two miles above Herkimer diverts most of the water from the West Canada Creek into an industrial canal which runs through Herkimer and joins the Mohawk about a half-mile west of the mouth of the West Canada proper.

*"Because of the large volume of water in the West Canada Creek , and because of the swiftness of the flow, the effects of the pollution from the various villages along the stream last only for a short distance. Pollution from Hinckley, Prospect and Trenton Falls is not enough to noticeably affect the invertebrate fauna (*insects and crayfish*) of the stream. Newport's pollution is slightly more serious than that of Poland , but in both cases any detrimental effect is probably offset by the enrichment of the stream fauna. The ulti-mate result of the pollution at Middleville may be considered the same as that from the villages just mentioned ; the immediate result, however, is quite different. The chief source of pollution is a tannery just above the Middleville bridge. Tannery wastes, including dyes, spent liquors, and a great amount of hair are released directly into the stream. Examination of the creek at the points where the tannery pollution enters showed an entire absence of invertebrate life for two hundred feet downstream along the east bank. In this area the hair and scrapings in many places cover the bottom for the depth of a foot."*

This report noted that the pollution from the Middleville tan-nery, high water temperatures and the diversion of water for the Herkimer industrial canal made the section from Middleville to the Mohawk River unsuitable for trout, although smallmouth bass, suckers and minnows were found there.

STOCKING RECOMMENDATIONS

General recommendations noted that because the falls at Wilmurt (north of Hinckley Lake) prevents such species as fallfish and perch from going upstream, only native brook trout should be stocked in the river and tributaries above the falls, thus maintaining the native fishery.

From Wilmurt to the dam at Hinckley rainbow trout were con-sidered the most tolerant of water conditions and the most likely to compete with fallfish and perch. Stocking 6-inch brook trout was also recommended.

UNUSUALLY FINE FOR TROUT

The stretch of water from below Hinckley Dam to the Trenton Gorge power dam was considered *"unusually fine for trout"* due to a constant flow of cold water from the bottom of the reservoir. On July 21, 1934 the water temperature was 63 degrees F when the air temperature was 82 degrees F in the gorge below the falls at Prospect. The stocking of rainbow trout and brook trout was recommended for this area where there was already a population of brown trout.

The section of the river below the power dam to the generation plant was deemed unsuitable for stocking trout due to the extreme water fluctuation.

BROWN TROUT REACHED GOOD SIZE HERE

Below the power plant, at the village of Trenton Falls all the way to Middleville , it was noted that water temperatures are favorable for trout. Brown trout reached good size here, despite the fact this area was heavily fished and smallmouth bass were present.Stocking 6-inch brown trout was recommended because of the heavy fishing pressure and to *"give the trout as much advantage as possible in their competition with the bass."*

BEST FOR BASS

From Middleville to the industrial canal diversion dam, where summer temperatures were not favorable to trout, smallmouth bass were present and continued stocking of bass was recommended.

From the diversion dam to the mouth of the river, a distance of approximately 2.6 miles, natural spawning of smallmouth bass was considered to be *"very successful."* It was noted that this spawning supplied fish for the Mohawk River, but few fish stayed in the West Canada because the draw down in this area was so great.

NO MORE WALLEYES OR LAKE TROUT

There was no mention of the previous stockings of lake trout in Hinckley Lake or walleye in the West Canada. Apparently the introductions of these species were unsuccessful. Bullhead stocking was also terminated, but was successful in establishing this species in the lake and some areas of the river.

LAKES, RIVER AND TRIBUTARIES GET THEIR SHARE

Two of the three West Canada Lakes were allocated generous stocking allotments. West Lake, the deepest, received 15,000 lake trout and 15,000 brook trout; South Lake received 10,000 brook trout, while Mud Lake was considered too shallow to hold fish year round.

Stretches of the main branch and most of the tributaries, between the source-lakes and Wilmurt, were allocated **brook trout** as follows:

West Canada (24.6 miles)—19,700 fish
Indian River (3 miles)—2,700
Metcalf Brook (7.4 miles)—4,700
Honondega Brook (3.7 miles)—4, 600
    Jones Brook (1.1 miles)—990
South Branch West Canada (17.2 miles)—15,500 (large size)
    T-Lake Creek (1.8 miles)—480;
    Alder Creek (10.1miles)—2200
Mill Creek - Nobleboro (2.1 miles)—420

From its source to the falls at Wilmurt more than 50,000 brook trout were allotted for the river and tributaries.

WATERSHED LAKES ALSO GET FISH

In addition to the source-lakes, the following lakes in the West Canada watershed also received fish:

Metcalf Lake (96 acres)—10,000 brookies
Big Rock Lake (70 acres)—4,000 brookies; 1,000 lake trout
T-Lake (38 acres)—2,000 brookies
G-Lake (77 acres)—10,000 brookies

BROOKIES AND RAINBOWS BELOW WILMURT FALLS

Downstream from Wilmurt to Hinckley Dam allotments were a mix of brook trout and rainbow trout.

West Canada (5 miles)—5,000 rainbows; 1500 brookies.
Four Mile Creek (15 miles)—4720 rainbows; 4850 brookies.
Black Creek and its many tributaries (60 miles)—6,000 rainbows and 14,000 brookies.
Small Tributaries north side of Hinckley Reservoir (12.25 miles)—400 rainbows; 2000 brookies.

HINCKLEY RESERVOIR (2800 acres)—25,000 rainbows (large size) 25,000 brookies (large size).

BROOKIES, BROWNS AND RAINBOWS
BELOW HINCKLEY

West Canada from Hinckley Dam to the power dam above Trenton Falls (4.1 miles)—10, 250 rainbows; 10,250 brookies.
West Canada from Power Plant to Middleville (19 miles)—95,000 brown trout.
West Canada from Middleville to Mouth (10 miles) too polluted, too warm, too low for trout.

TRIBUTARIES BELOW TRENTON FALLS

Cincinnati Creek (was Steuben Creek all the way to West Canada back then) (15.5 miles)—7,250 brown trout
    Steuben Creek (9 miles)—1,800 browns.
Dover Rd Brook (3.75 miles)—1,000 browns.
Mill Creek—polluted to Gravesville
    (2.1 mile above falls)—370 brookies.
Cold Brook (7.8 miles)—2,200 brookies.
Terry Brook (2.4 miles)—240 brookies.
Shed Brook—above falls (1.5 miles)—270 browns.
White Creek upper stretch (4 miles)—1,080 brookies.
    Tributaries (4 miles)—1,300 brookies.
City Brook , upper, Wolf Hollow Brook (1.6 miles)—570 browns.
Fishing Rock Stream, upper (1 mile)—270 browns.
Maltanner Creek—none—too warm, too dry.
Stony Creek—none—too dry.
North Creek—none—too warm, too dry.

The Survey Report emphasized the need to stock 6-inch trout—the legal size limit at the time—in the areas where trout had to compete with other fish and where angler pressure was greatest.

These yearly stocking levels were maintained at 85–90 percent of recommendation in most West Canada waters into the 1960s, with occasional lapses because of lack of funds and elimination of some waters due to restricted (posting) access.

BEST OF THE BEST LOST IN 1959

In 1959 Niagara Mohawk Power Corporation built a dam above the falls at Prospect. This was the death knell for one of the best stretches of trout water in New York State. The boulder strewn stream between Hinckley and Prospect that the 1934 Survey recognized as *"unusually fine for trout"* was covered by Prospect Pond (Lower Hinckley Lake). Local trout anglers were devastated.

The stream below the Prospect dam all the way to Trenton Falls was also lost to trout fishing. Except during the spring runoff and other high water periods, West Canada waters bypassed the falls and gorge at Prospect through a canal that led to the new Prospect Power Plant. And, because of a number of fatal accidents in the Trenton Gorge (not fishermen) and subsequent lawsuits, the entire gorge was posted by the power company.

PROSPECT POND—A NEW FISHERY

In 1960 the State stocked Prospect Pond with 2,000 yearling and 2,500 fingerling rainbow trout each year until 1963 when the allocation was changed to 2,000 rainbow and 2,100 brown trout yearlings. This stocking continued through 1974. Except for some "where-they-were-dumped-in" success, these stockings did not produce "good fishing" in the Pond, although some large trout were caught each year below the dam at Hinckley.

The reported fishing in Prospect Pond was so poor no fish were stocked in 1975 and 1976. Stocking resumed in 1977 but with a twist. Tagged rainbows and browns were put in the Pond for three years. The results of this "Tagging Study" indicated that stocked fish were surviving and local anglers were learning how to catch them. Since then 2,000 rainbow and 2,000 brown trout yearlings have been stocked each year. Browns and rainbows in the 2–5 pound class are common catches here, especially below the Hinckley Dam. (This year—1997—350 two-year old, 15-inch brown trout will be stocked in Prospect Pond.)

HINCKLEY LAKE A LOST CAUSE?

As far back as the 1930s Hinckley Reservoir was recognized as an infertile body of water that was poor fish habitat. The 1935 Survey noted that all of the fish species studied were stunted, and snails, aquatic insects and crustacea were practically absent. However, because so many people fished the reservoir—many of them remembering the short-lived "good old days"—the State continued to stock Hinckley with browns and rainbows to provide fish for a "demanding public". Most of these fish were caught soon after they were put in the lake or at the mouths of tributary streams in the spring. From time to time when the lake was low and warm during the summer, the coldest tributaries attracted trout in considerable numbers.

Prior to 1970, intentionally or by accident (a washed out pond perhaps) chain pickerel were put in the lake, and for several years these predators multiplied and were frequently caught in Hinckley and Prospect Pond.

In 1971 a proposal by a young outdoor writer (the author) and a public-support meeting at the Hinckley Hotel, to stock walleyes in Hinckley Lake was considered by the New York State Department of Environmental Conservation (DEC). In the spring of 1972, 402 adult walleyes were stocked in the upper end of the lake. Many of these fish died after the first day. Some were removed by local "fish bandits" while they were still in shallow water.

In 1973, 400 more adult, tagged walleyes were stocked. Many died within a few days. In 1974 and 75, 10 million walleye fry were put in the lake. Only a dozen tags from the adult fish were returned to DEC and no reports of smaller fish were ever received.

The failure of this and previous efforts to make Hinckley a good place to fish, inspired the first comprehensive study of the lake since 1935. DEC conducted a Hinckley Reservoir Survey in 1976. Citing previous studies of the lake bottom and water quality, and their year long biological survey, DEC concluded that Hinckley would never be a good fishery.

The lake bottom is over 80% sand, 10–15 percent small gravel and 5% clay and rock. This bottom strata holds almost none of the nutrients needed to sustain a healthy fish population. (At the extreme—no nutrients, no little critters to feed little fish, no little fish to feed big fish.)

Making this situation even worse is the fact that the river, tributary streams and other runoffs, which flow through Adirondack rock and soils, are very low in nutrients.

Because the reservoir's function is to control downstream flooding and provide water for the Barge Canal and for generating electrical power, it's drawn down in the winter prior to spring flooding, and sometimes drawn down in the summer to provide water for the canal and power plants. These draw-downs and subsequent high water flushings remove most of the nutrients from the lake.

Almost all of the fish caught in the nets during the 1976 Survey were stunted when compared to the fish in other northern New York lakes. Although trout, pickerel, fallfish, suckers, bullheads, sunfish and minnows were taken during the survey, not one walleye was netted.

The discovery that there were almost no zooplankton (the little critters that walleye fry eat)) in the lake explains why walleye fry didn't survive, but no one knows what happened to the adult walleyes. Perhaps the walleye's intolerance of even low levels of acidity is the answer.

Today, Hinckley Lake remains a poor fishery, although some good catches of trout are caught in the spring of the year at the mouths of tributary streams.

FISHING FRENZY IN 95

In the summer of 1995 during unusually low water conditions and a long spell of hot weather, for the first time ever recorded, the lake didn't stratify. Because there was no cold water at the bottom of the lake, almost the entire trout population moved into spring-fed tributary streams to find comfortable water. For a few weeks this mass migration of trout created a fishing bonanza. Anglers took hundreds of fish from such waters as the brook at Cookinhams Bay. Some anglers took many times their limit. Fortunately some of them were caught and fined. The resulting publicity helped to slow down the fishing frenzy.

MAJOR SHIFT IN MANAGEMENT OF FISHERY

In the 1970s a major shift in philosophy occurred among fisheries managers in New York State. With the support of such organizations as the New York State Conservation Council and Trout Unlimited, quality fishing replaced quantity fishing as the goal of fisheries management in many waters. This change in management philosophy, subsequent studies of fish growth and survival, and changes in water quality, had a dramatic impact on the stocking programs and fishing in West Canada waters.

A number of studies indicated that stocking too many fish resulted in stunted fish, and in some areas, caused a decline in natural production. Other studies revealed that larger fish survived better than smaller fish, and that in areas where water temperatures were high during the summer months and/or acidity was on the increase, few stocked fish survived the first year.

By the mid 70's almost all stocking of the river, tributaries and lakes in the headwaters of the West Canada was terminated. Stocking continued from the Nobleboro to Hinckley Dam but was significantly reduced. In 1979, 8,000 browns, 11,700 brookies and 3,000 rainbows were stocked here. All stocking of rainbow trout ended in this area in 1983 because of poor survival due to acid rain. Throughout the 80's and into the 90's this area received 2500 brown trout and 6100 brook trout each year.

QUALITY NOT QUANTITY ON THE LOWER RIVER

In 1975 a "three trout, 12-inch limit, artificial lures only" Special Regulations Section was established from the Trenton Falls Bridge to the mouth of Cincinnati Creek. From 1967 to 1976 the stocking rate in the river below Trenton Falls had been reduced from 120,000 to 88,900 brown trout. In 1977 it was further reduced to 50,100. The stage was set for quality fishing in the lower West Canada Creek.

Further studies in this section of the river indicated there was practically no natural production of trout in the river due to fluctuating water levels caused by power generation requirements and lack of proper-sized gravel spawning areas. During the winter the low cycle of this fluctuating water exposed large areas to cold temperatures and caused "anchor ice" to form on river-bottom rocks, freezing potential spawning and feeding areas, and killing all animal life exposed to it.

Stocked fish, however, survived and grew to good size if stocking levels were not too high. Other studies noted the natural production of brook trout in many tributary streams and brown trout in Cincinnati Creek.

In the 1980s stocking levels in the river were further reduced to 45,500 brown trout per year, and except for the nutrient rich Cincinnati, which receives 3,900 browns, all tributary stream stocking was terminated.

FEWER FISH—BIGGER FISH

While the number of fish stocked decreased, the size of these fish has increased. Nine and 10-inch fish have been stocked in recent years. Angler interviews on the West Canada and elseware in the state indicate that most trout fishermen would rather catch a few big fish than several small fish. Fishery Biologists point out that two ten-inch fish provide more meat than several 6-inchers. In 1997 an experimental stocking of 2800 two-year old, 15-inch fish will be put in the river from Trenton Falls to Herkimer.

BIG-TROUT WATER

Just 10 years ago a foot-long trout taken from the lower river was considered a good catch. A 20-inch fish was an exceptional trophy. Today 12-15- inch fish are quite common, 20-inch fish are taken regularly by a few good anglers, and a 25-inch fish is an exceptional trophy. Improved water quality, strict regulation of stream flow and reduced stocking levels have all contributed to creating this big-trout fishery. Equally important is the growing number of fishermen who release fish "to fight another day".

NO KILL SECTION IN 1997–98

The success of "No Kill" areas on other major trout waters in New York State have resulted in numerous requests for DEC to create a section on the West Canada where anglers can fish with lures and flies, but must release all trout. All signs point to the Special Trout Section from the Trenton Falls Bridge to the mouth of Cincinnati Creek as becoming "No Kill" in October 1997.

LOST AND FOUND TROUT WATER

About the time all the changes were taking place in fisheries management philosophy, the tannery in Middleville closed, the New York State Pure Waters Act required major improvements in sewage and waste disposal ..... and 10 more miles of trout water were added to West Canada Creek.

Additional sewage cleanup and better regulation of waterflow from Hinckley Lake and the power dams along the river, have helped make this stretch of water one of the West Canada's best kept secrets. This "found" trout water helped make up for the "lost" trout water between Hinckley and Prospect.

NEW HOPE FOR TRIBUTARIES AND THE UPPER RIVER

While no one expects the tributaries or the upper river to return to "the good old days" of natural production or heavy stocking, there are signs of improvement. Natural production of brook trout has been noted all the way from the source-lakes to the lower valley tributaries.

For the first time in many years, anglers who hike into West Canada Lakes have reported good catches of brook trout at the outlet of Mud Lake in the Spring. Water quality—reduced acidity—has improved so much that DEC plans to stock brook trout in both Mud Lake and South Lake in 1997. They also plan to study the acidity of West Lake for possible future stocking. Other West Canada watershed lakes that will be stocked are Bear Lake, Beaver Dam Pond, Metcalf Lake, Poor Lake and Spruce Lake.

BASS AND FALLFISH STILL IN THE RIVER

Although the West Canada is managed as a trout fishery, smallmouth bass are still in the river. Twelve-inch bass are quite common and many 16-inchers are caught every year. While bass are found all the way up to Trenton Falls, the slower waters below Comstock Bridge all the way to the Mohawk River are the most productive and provide a number of natural spawning areas. Until recently no bass were found above Trenton Falls, however, there are some recent reports of bass in Prospect Pond and Hinckley Lake.

Wherever there are trout and bass there are fallfish. These giant minnows—that can grow to 2 pounds —- were once restricted to the lower river, however, they are now well established in West Canada waters all the way up to Wilmurt Falls. Black Creek has long been a fallfish spawning area.

AFTER 200 YEARS

Much has happened to the West Canada and its tributaries in the past 200 years. Pristine waters were used and abused, damned and polluted, and then cleaned and controlled. Fish thrived, fish died, and thrived again. Legendary trout waters were lost, others gained, some reborn. Fisheries management changed from stocking hundreds of thousands of little fish to stocking thousands of big fish; from stocking fish in every lake and every stream to putting them where they survive and grow, and don't compete with naturally spawning fish. Indeed, the West Canada has been an up and down, down and up fishery these past 200 years.

Chapter 3
Lower River
PREMIER TROUT WATER

The 29 miles of the West Canada from Trenton Falls to Herkimer offers more access to good brown trout water than any stream in the state. More than 45,000 browns are stocked here every year, most of them 9-inch fish. The West Canada in this lower valley is such good trout growing water, these stocked fish become 10 and 12 inchers in a single season. The holdover and growth rates are so high 17–20-inch fish are quite common, and a few 25-inch plus fish are taken. In 1996 a 27-1/2-inch, 8-pound brown was taken by a bait fisherman above the dam at Newport. Fly fishermen have caught and released fish of this size in the past couple of years in different stretches of the river.

Brook trout are also in the river, although they are not stocked by the state. They come from feeder streams where they reproduce naturally. About three years ago, I caught a 13-inch brookie from a river-pool near the mouth of Mill Creek, and I've caught smaller brookies near the mouth of other creeks along the river. In the summer of 1996 I spent a morning with a DEC crew that was conducting a fish-shocking survey in the river below Poland. In a stretch of out-of -the-way fast water they took a dozen trout, half of them were brookies.

Rainbow trout are no longer stocked in the river, except for Prospect Pond, yet in 1996 a number of fishermen reported catching rainbow trout below Trenton Falls and near Newport. Rainbows that came down from Prospect Pond and a farm pond that washed out along White Creek may account for these fish.

Smallmouth bass are not abundant the length of the river, but in some areas 12-inch fish are common, with a good number of 15-inch fish taken every year. A few 19-inch bass have been reported. Most of the good bass waters are in the slow-water stretches between Comstock Bridge and Newport with one of the best spots being along the "wall" at Newport. There is also good smallmouth water in the river below Middleville. Although most deeper stillwaters hold fish, the power dam below Kast Bridge, the old power station dam at Herkimer and the pools near and at the mouth of the river are usually the most productive.

Fallfish are everywhere in the river where there are trout or bass, and they take any lure, fly or bait a trout or bass will. Fallfish hit hard, but don't fight as long as a trout or bass. A 10-incher is a good size fish, although 16-inch fallfish are caught every season. When trout or bass have lockjaw, fallfish can save the day by providing all the action there is on the river.

Walleyes are found at the mouth of the river and in the deeper pools up to the first dam. Some other fish in the river are rock bass, sunfish, perch, chubs and even largemouth bass. Most of these fish are caught in the deeper pools and around dams.

I was canoe-fishing a deep pool above Poland where I had previously caught brown trout, brook trout and smallmouth bass. While untangling line and crankbait from my rod tip, I drifted by the hole and missed the best place to cast. Just below the pool was a scum-covered backset, so I flipped the crankbait into it. A fish took the lure and leaped out of the water. It was a 2-1/2 pound largemouth. Must have washed out of a nearby pond.

ACCESS, ACCESS, EVERYWHERE ACCESS

It's amazing how much of the West Canada can be fished from shore or by wading the river. Although most stretches run through private property, fishing is permitted on long stretches of the river by Fish and Wildlife Management Act agreements with landowners, Public Fishing Rights easements or by the NYS Department of Transportation.

FWMA agreements with landowners give anglers the *privilege* to fish specific stretches of stream. These agreements are not permanent and can be cancelled. All of the FWMA fishing areas on the West Canada are between Trenton Falls and the Comstock Bridge.

Public Fishing Rights areas are permanent easements purchased by the state that extend along the riverbank to the middle of the stream. Easements are also purchased to provide parking areas and access points for fishermen. "Public Fishing" signs are posted every 300 feet along the shoreline. There are numerous Public Fishing Rights areas on the West Canada between Comstock Bridge and Herkimer.

James Klosek caught this 25-inch, 9-year old brown trout on a Rapala from West Canada Creek on the opening day of trout season in 1995. (photo courtesy of James Klosek)

DOT lands along the West Canada are near bridges, where the river and roads run side by side and along a section of the old railroad bed in the Kast Bridge—Herkimer area. Incidentally, although the railroad bed from Poland to below Middleville is privately owned, it's not posted in most areas and provides an excellent way to reach stretches of the river that few fishermen ever see.

Refer to map panels for location of parking areas, access sites, stretches of the river where fishing is permitted, the route of the abandoned railroad bed and other access roads and trails.

In addition to the streamside access noted above, the entire stream comes under the Rights of Passage laws that allow fishing from a canoe or boat. (See Chapter 9 for information on the best and safest places to float the lower river.)

TRENTON FALLS TO HERKIMER

It's difficult to choose the best places to fish on the lower West Canada; there are just so many good places to choose from. It's become even more difficult in recent years since DEC and the managers of all the dams on the river have worked so closely to maintain a significant waterflow throughout the year. Areas that were once marginal or poor trout water, hold some very good fish.

If time and abilities restrict you to roadside fishing, there are plenty of places to fish in this area. If getting away from the road and into some seldom-fished water is what you prefer, there are literally miles of water you can fish from shore, by wading or from a canoe. The following by no means covers every good fishing spot on the river, however, with this information and associated map panels, it will point you in the right direction.

SPECIAL WATER—NO KILL FISHING

The most pristine stretch of water on the lower river is the 2.5 miles from Trenton Falls to the mouth of Cincinnati Creek. Here rapids, runs, riffs and pools abound, away from the road. There are steep banks, islands, huge rocks and overhanging trees, with a few old homesteads mixed in. Foot-long trout are common and a few 20-inchers are taken each year.

With such names as *Banoch's Riff, Poor Man's Pool, Stedson's Pool, Barking Dog Run, The Door Knocker, Paradise, Blue Barn Bend, High Bank* and *Mal's Rock*, this is the kind of water trout fishermen dream about. This is also the section that was designated "Special Trout Water" in 1975. Anglers could take only three trout over 12 inches on lures. Starting October 1997 this special stretch of river will become "No Kill" water. Perhaps 20-inch fish will be common here in years to come. *(See also Chapter 2.)*

BIG HOLES, DEEP RUNS, BIG FISH

The river downstream from Cincinnati Creek may not be pristine in most places and anglers can keep what they catch on lures, flies or bait, but make no mistake, this is still good trout water.

The pool on *Power's Bend*, just below the mouth of the Cincinnati is a popular roadside fishing spot, and just downstream *Bianco's Riff* is a fly fishing favorite. The deep pool at *Ryan's Bend* is another streamside favorite as is the stretch of water above the Fishermen's Parking Area at Comstock Bridge.

Below Comstock Bridge all the way to the mouth of Mill Creek, the river widens, runs deep and slows to a snail's pace. Here begins *The Lake*, one of the longest stretches of big-fish

A deep hole filled with boulders and a plug that looks like a cray-fish produced this fat brookie.

water on the river. More 20-inch plus browns have come from this boulder-bottom water than from any area except perhaps Borden's Bay. Big brookies and smallmouths are also caught here.

Except for the upper and lower ends most of *The Lake* is difficult, if not impossible, to fish from shore or by wading. The best way to fish here is from a canoe or small boat.

Just downstream from The Lake are some riffs around three islands. The pools below the islands hold fish, as do the runs and big rocks from there to the old Cameron Covered Bridge abutments. These reminders of a gone-by era almost always produce a nice trout or bass. The downstream pool holds some very good fish.

Longtime friend and legendary fly fisherman, Jack McDiarmid used to come here often. He was 87 when he took a 22-inch brown from the *Cameron Bridge Pool* on his favorite fly, a Royal Coachman. Jack has passed on but he will always be remembered as Mr. West Canada Creek.

Downstream from the bridge pool is a stretch of stream known as *Yellow Gate*, named after the gate at the fishermen's access road off Route 28 which leads to a parking and Fishing Rights Area. As allowed by law, the current landowner has posted this area for fishing only. So, it cannot be used for launching canoes, camping or picnicking. A laundry list of "can't dos" is posted near the yellow gate, that is located almost across from Beecher Road.

Boulder Run is just upstream from the new "Crescent Bridge" where Route 28 intersects with Route 8. A huge oft-painted, mid-stream boulder and a new paved parking area mark this roadside stretch of water that has long been popular with fishermen.

The deep waters near the bridge abutments hold big trout and smallmouth bass. Bass and fallfish lurk in the long "bays" in this area.

Another roadside parking area along Route 8/28, on the down-stream side of the new bridge, overlooks Sunny Island and provides access to the riffs and pools in this area. *Oxbow Bend* holds many small fish and a few big guys, especially along the riprapp on the east side of the river where overhanging trees provide shade in the heat of the day. This usually deep water is best fished from a canoe.

Bat Run is just downstream from the Poland Bridge, where there's another new Fishermen's Parking Area. At times this run holds a great many stocked trout and in the deeper water, some big fish.

Some very good smallmouth bass water begins just below Bat Run and continues all the way to the *Lumberyard Pool* in back of Poland. I was fishing with Mark Eychner when he caught a 16-inch smallmouth in this area, and I've caught a number of 12–14-inch bass here. Trees lying in the water and mid-stream boulders produced most of these fish. This deep water stretch of the West Canada also holds some big browns.

The *Lumberyard Pool* (the lumberyard closed years ago) holds some fine brown trout plus some brook trout that were born and bred in Cold Brook. This is not public fishing water, but it's not posted and local youngsters take some nice fish out of this pool each year.

With overhanging evergreens and rippling waters, the West Canada from Poland to within sight of the Old State Road Bridge, could be on any wilderness stream, if not for the remnants of old industry on the east side of the river. The bridge (closed in 1995, demolished in '96 and under construction in '97), downstream pools and the mid-stream abutment of a long-abandoned bridge are popu-lar fishing spots in this area.

The waters near the Fishermen's Parking Area off Route 28 below Poland is without a doubt the most popular fishing spot in the entire river. Early in the season, entire families line the bank to fish this *Parking Lot Pool*. Most of these early-season anglers are bait

> **WARNING:** *The river level fluctuates with the needs of the power generating plants. Generally, water is released in the morning at Trenton Falls around 9 a.m. and moves down the river about 5 miles per hour, reaching the mouth of the stream in late afternoon. This high water is great for canoeists and kayakers, especially during low water periods, but it can be dangerous to wading fishermen who are not prepared.*

fishermen, but later in the season this area is also popular with spin and fly fishermen. Upstream boulders hold fish, as do the downstream pool and tail waters. Both sides of the river are Public Fishing Rights areas. Some of the most successful fishermen hike into the seldom-fished water opposite the parking area. Or they fish it from a canoe or small boat.

DANGEROUS WATER, GOOD FISHING

The quiet, almost serene waters of the *Parking Lot Pool* and the shoreline evergreens along *Carpenter's Bend* hide the sight and sound of one of the most dangerous rapids on the river. Canoeists have been sucked into these rapids during high-water periods. Some of them made it through, having experienced a thrill of a lifetime. Others have been injured and a few have lost their lives. This two-mile stretch of river is a place to avoid during the spring runoff and other high-water periods, but a good place to fish the rest of the fishing season.

The pools and quiet-water near boulders and rock shelves hold some very nice fish the length of the rapids, as does the seemingly flat-water just above Paul's Island. Experienced fishermen know this run is not flat below the surface, but features a number of bottom depressions that hold some nice fish. This "pocket water" is one of the most difficult areas to fish on the river. When the water is clear and easy to wade, a fish can usually see a fisherman long before he's within casting range. I've talked to fly fishermen who have cast for hours at trout they could see in these pockets without taking a single fish.

To a few dedicated West Canada fishermen this water is their greatest challenge. John Bianco has cast flies here for years and although he's caught many good fish, one an 8-pound brown trout taken on a Haystack fly in the fall of '95, he has fished here many nights without raising a single fish.

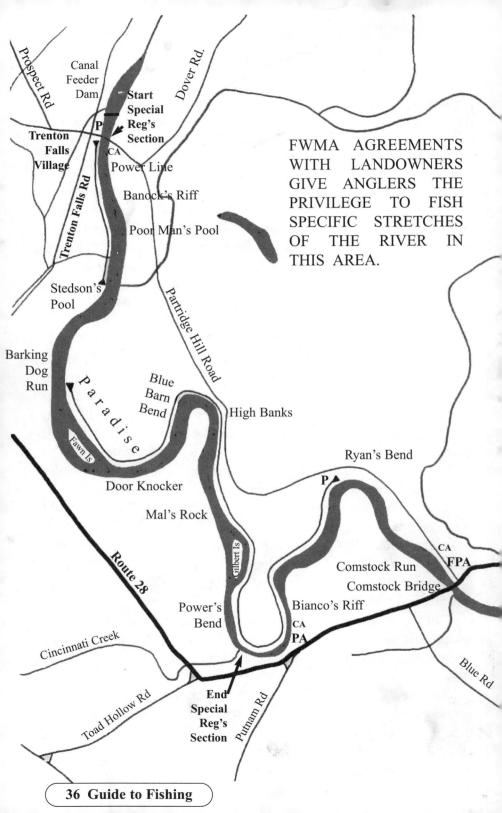

Prospect Rd

Canal
Feeder
Dam

Dover Rd.

**Start
Special
Reg's
Section**

P

**Trenton
Falls
Village**

CA

Power Line

Trenton Falls Rd

Banock's Riff

Poor Man's Pool

FWMA AGREEMENTS
WITH LANDOWNERS
GIVE ANGLERS THE
PRIVILEGE TO FISH
SPECIFIC STRETCHES
OF THE RIVER IN
THIS AREA.

Stedson's
Pool

Barking
Dog
Run

Partridge Hill Road

P a r a d i s e

Fawn Is

Blue
Barn
Bend

High Banks

Ryan's Bend

P

Door Knocker

Mal's Rock

Gilbert Is

Route 28

CA
FPA

Comstock Run

Comstock Bridge

Bianco's Riff

Power's
Bend

CA
PA

Cincinnati Creek

Toad Hollow Rd

Putnam Rd

**End
Special
Reg's
Section**

Blue Rd

36 **Guide to Fishing**

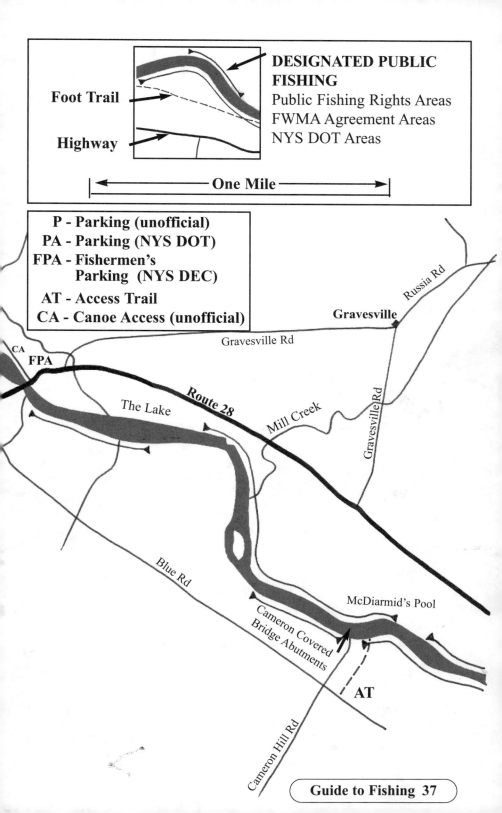

DESIGNATED PUBLIC
FISHING
Public Fishing Rights Areas
FWMA Agreement Areas
NYS DOT Areas

Foot Trail

Highway

One Mile

P - Parking (unofficial)
PA - Parking (NYS DOT)
FPA - Fishermen's
      Parking (NYS DEC)
AT - Access Trail
CA - Canoe Access (unofficial)

Russia Rd

Gravesville

Gravesville Rd

CA
FPA

Route 28

The Lake

Mill Creek

Gravesville Rd

Blue Rd

McDiarmid's Pool

Cameron Covered
Bridge Abutments

AT

Cameron Hill Rd

Guide to Fishing 37

West Canada Creek is the boundary line between Oneida County and Herkimer County from Hinckley to Poland.

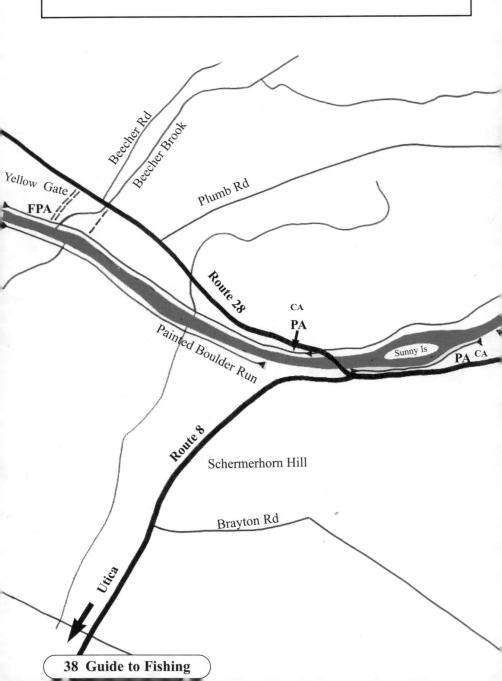

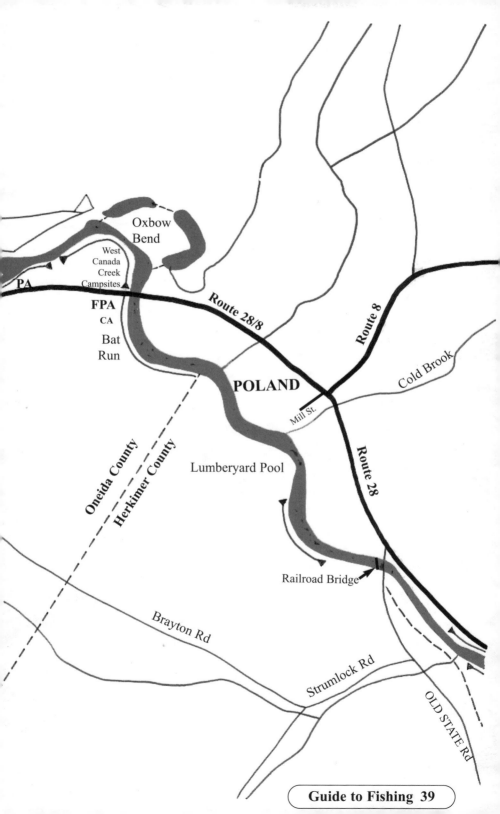

Oxbow
Bend

West
Canada
Creek
Campsites

PA

FPA

CA

Bat
Run

Route 28/8

Route 8

Cold Brook

POLAND

Mill St.

Oneida County

Herkimer County

Lumberyard Pool

Route 28

Railroad Bridge

Brayton Rd

Strumlock Rd

OLD STATE Rd

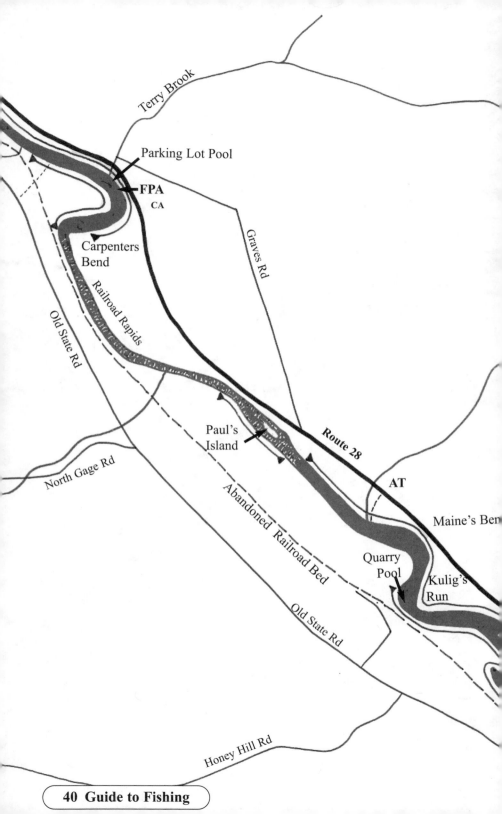

Terry Brook

Parking Lot Pool

FPA
CA

Carpenters
Bend

Railroad Rapids

Graves Rd

Old State Rd

Paul's
Island

Route 28

AT

North Gage Rd

Maine's Ber

Abandoned Railroad Bed

Quarry
Pool

Kulig's
Run

Old State Rd

Honey Hill Rd

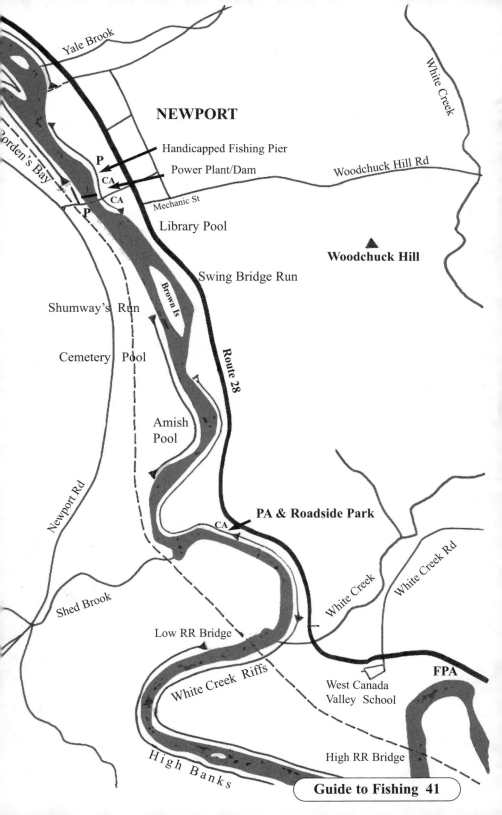

Yale Brook

White Creek

NEWPORT

orden's Bay

Handicapped Fishing Pier

P

CA

Power Plant/Dam

Woodchuck Hill Rd

CA

P

Mechanic St

Library Pool

Woodchuck Hill

Swing Bridge Run

Brown Is

Shumway's Run

Cemetery Pool

Route 28

Amish Pool

Newport Rd

PA & Roadside Park

CA

Shed Brook

White Creek

White Creek Rd

Low RR Bridge

White Creek

White Creek Riffs

West Canada Valley School

FPA

High Banks

High RR Bridge

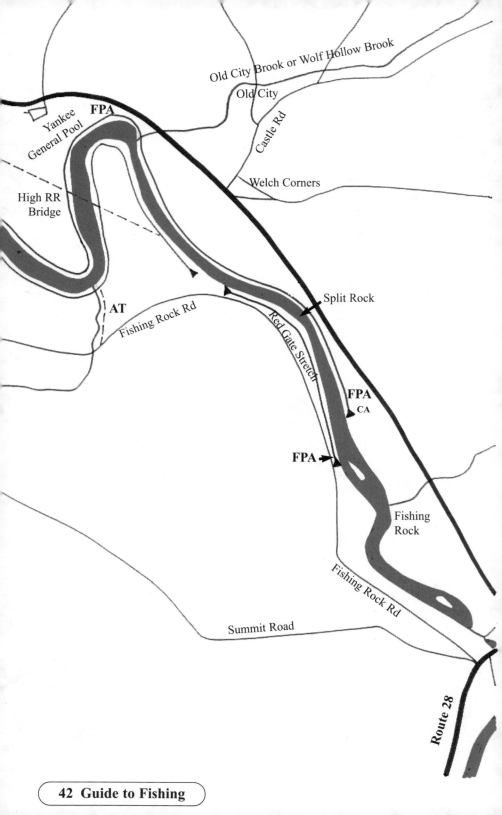

Old City Brook or Wolf Hollow Brook

Old City

Castle Rd

Yankee
General Pool

FPA

Welch Corners

High RR
Bridge

AT

Fishing Rock Rd

Split Rock

Red Gate Stretch

FPA
CA

FPA

Fishing
Rock

Fishing Rock Rd

Summit Road

Route 28

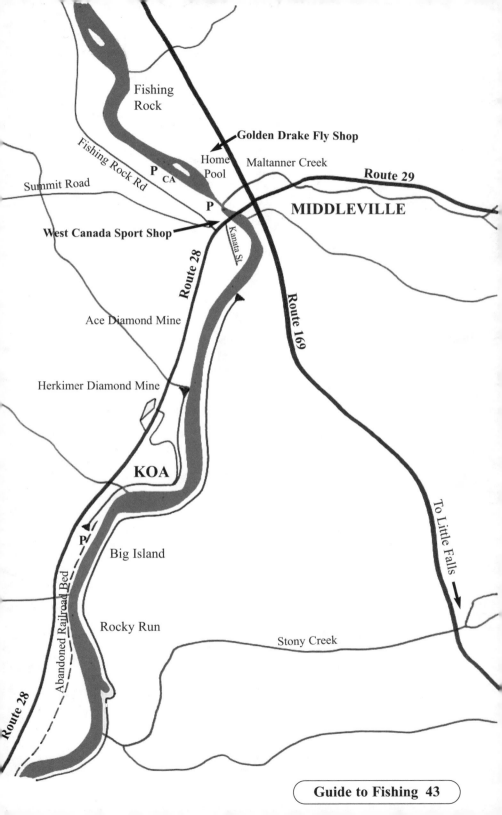

Fishing Rock

Golden Drake Fly Shop

Fishing Rock Rd

Summit Road

P CA

Home Pool

Maltanner Creek

Route 29

P

MIDDLEVILLE

West Canada Sport Shop

Kanata St.

Route 28

Ace Diamond Mine

Route 169

Herkimer Diamond Mine

KOA

To Little Falls

P

Big Island

Abandoned Railroad Bed

Rocky Run

Stony Creek

Route 28

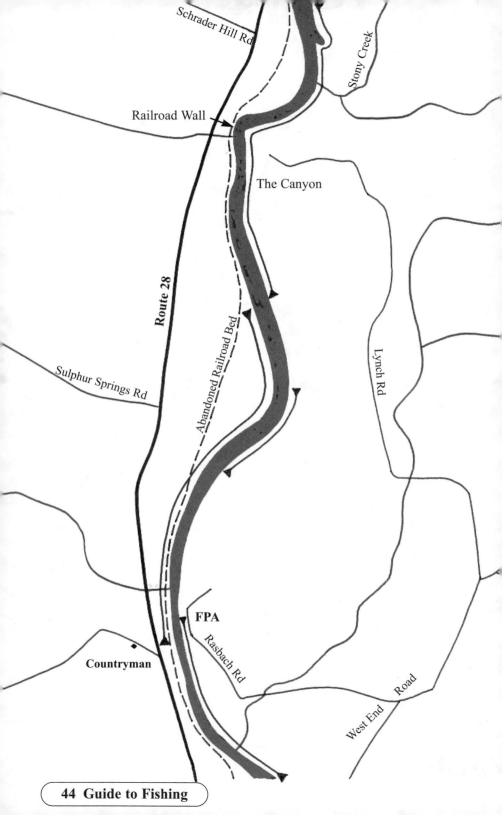

Schrader Hill Rd

Stony Creek

Railroad Wall →

The Canyon

Route 28

Lynch Rd

Sulphur Springs Rd

Abandoned Railroad Bed

FPA

Rasbach Rd

Countryman

West End Road

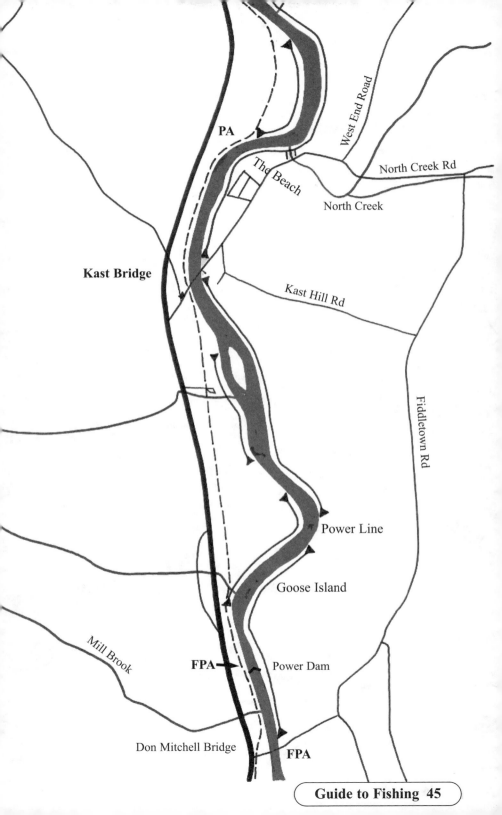

PA

West End Road

North Creek Rd

The Beach

North Creek

Kast Bridge

Kast Hill Rd

Fiddletown Rd

Power Line

Goose Island

Mill Brook

FPA → Power Dam

Don Mitchell Bridge

FPA

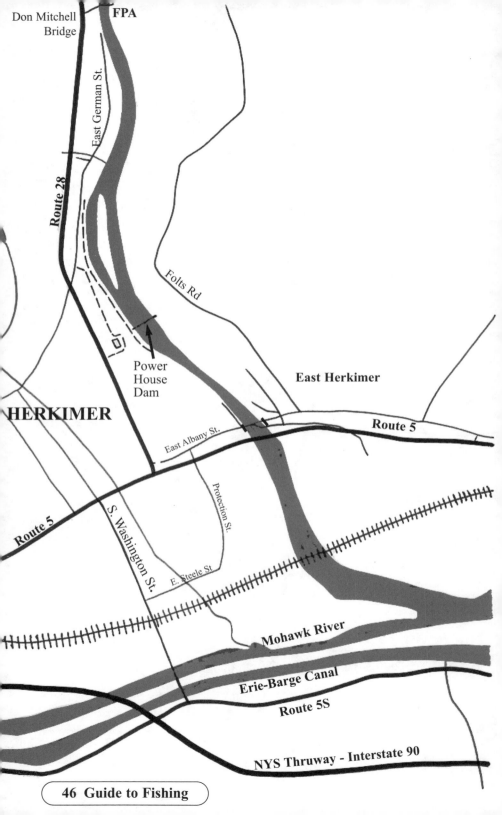

Don Mitchell
Bridge

FPA

East German St.

Route 28

Folts Rd

Power
House
Dam

HERKIMER

East Herkimer

East Albany St.

Route 5

Route 5

S. Washington St.

Protection St.

E. Steele St

Mohawk River

Erie-Barge Canal

Route 5S

NYS Thruway - Interstate 90

BOULDERS, RUNS, DEEP POOLS AND BORDEN'S BAY

There's a nice pool on the west side of Paul's Island that is almost always good for a fish or two, but it's the boulder-strewn water from below the island all the way to *Maine's Bend* that holds the most fish in this area. The runs on both sides and downstream from the islands at Maine's Bend are sometimes loaded with small trout.

There are some big fish in *Quarry Pool* and downstream in Kulig's *Run.* I've caught dozens of small trout here and lost a couple of 14–15-inch fish on ultralight spinning tackle while fishing from a canoe. This is one of Randy Kulig's favorite runs to cast flies for big browns. He and a few of his customers at the Golden Drake Fly Shop in Middleville have taken some good fish from this exceptional water.

One of the reasons it's so exceptional is the deep-water pond just downstream. There's been a dam at Newport since the early 1800s where it provided water for mills and factories for over 150 years. The last factory to close was the Borden Instant Coffee Plant, hence the name, *Borden's Bay.* Today the dam serves a power generating plant.

There's a Handicap Accessible Fishermen's Platform on the east side of the river, but most of the big fish are caught by bank fishermen off the stone wall on the west side near the old coffee plant. This is the spot where a 27-1/2-inch brown was taken in the spring of 96, and where some 15–16-inch smallmouths are caught every year. There are plenty of places to park in this area, on both sides of the river.

Just downstream from the Newport Bridge, which by the way was built in 1853, the river's dolomite bottom was cut deep to provide better outflow for the power dam. This deep run is a relatively new fish haven.

Just upstream from the tree-covered Brown Island, which was once Newport's ball field, is *Library Pool* . On the east side of the island near the old suspension bridge abutments is *Swing Bridge Run*, and on the west side is *Shumway Run.* There are times, albeit rare, when all three of these fish havens hold feeding fish.

Downstream from the island is *Cemetery Pool*, followed by the *Amish Barn Pool* and the mouth of Shed Brook. The roadside park between Route 28 and the river provides access to the Public Fishing Rights stretches on the east side of the river. The railroad bed provides access on the other side. The area next to the park is heavily fished. Look for the coldwater spring that runs into the river upstream from the parking area. It can be a hotspot when the river is low and warm, or very cold.

Just below the parking area is the mouth of White Creek and the beginning of one of the finest stretches of big-trout water on the river. Very few fishermen have even seen this long stretch of away-from-the-road water because it's not easy to get to and some stretches are difficult if not impossible to wade. *White Creek Riffs* start at the *Low Bridge* and end at the first bend above *The High Banks,* where some monster trout lie. Around the bend is *High Bridge* and *Yankee General Pool.*

Access to this Public Fishing Area is through the West Canada Valley School grounds, from the railroad bed and from the Fishermen's Parking area along Route 28, next to the Yankee General Store/Restaurant.

The next downstream Fishermen's Parking Area on the Route 28 side of the river is about a half mile past Welch Corners, just below the rock quarry. From here you can fish *Split Rock* upstream and *Fishing Rock* downstream. Fishing Rock is the only outcrop of "Adirondack" granite on the lower West Canada. I have stood on this rock and caught brown trout from one side and smallmouth bass from the other. You can also get to this stretch of river from the Fishermen's Parking Area on the east side of the river along Fishing Rock Road.

Just below the remnants of an old power dam in Middleville is a deep hole that Randy Kulig, for obvious reasons, calls the *Home Pool.* His house (and now fly shop) was the first dwelling in Middleville to receive power from this old power dam.

A LONG WAY FROM THE BIG LAKE BUT STILL FISHY

Although releases from dams along the river provide a continuous flow of water below Middleville, it's a long way from the cold waters of Hinckley Lake and Prospect Pond. Also, long stretches of this part of the river are shallow and spread out, so they heat quickly in the summer sun. Definitely not brook trout water. Fortunately a number of deep holes and runs, a couple of downstream dams, plus lots and lots of rapids, provide enough cool, oxygenated water to support a good population of brown trout and smallmouth bass.

Because this is relatively new trout water *(See Chapter 2),* fishermen are still discovering the best places to fish. Some of the better fish havens are *Big Island, Rocky Run, and The Canyon.* Huge

Mark Eychner caught this big smallmouth bass from under a fallen tree near the village of Poland. It took a Rapala minnow.

rocks, rapids, stone walls (that support the old railroad bed), fallen trees, and stream outlets from both sides of the river, hold trout in this area. Much of it can be reached by walking the railroad bed.

A Fishermen's Parking Area on the east side of the river opposite Countryman provides access to the Public Fishing water in this area. Downstream is another parking area and a riverside gravel road on DOT land where the river was rerouted to eliminate two bridges on Route 28. *The Beach* is a deep hole that holds some good brown trout.

Almost every trout stream in upstate New York has a *Power Line Hole* and the West Canada is no exception. It and the waters around a gravel bar called *Goose Island* also hold some good fish. There's a Fishermen's Parking Area at the Power Generation Plant. I know of one 21-inch brown that was taken below the generators, and bigger fish were seen here in the past couple of years.

Just downstream from the power plant, at the east end of the Don Mitchell Bridge, is another Fishermen's Parking Area. Downstream, at the site of an old bridge, is *The Wall*. Fifty years ago there was just a trickle of water in this area; it was all directed from the upstream dam to the Hydraulic Canal to power mills and factories in Herkimer. Today there are trout and bass in this area of the river.

LAST DAM ON THE RIVER

The last dam on the West Canada before it reaches the Mohawk is behind an old coal power plant. This dam and a half mile of stream can be reached by walking the trail behind the power plant. Trout, bass, walleye and panfish are caught in this area. Rows of trees and high banks hide the sight and sounds of traffic, so it's hard to believe this area is right in Herkimer. For many longtime West Canada anglers, it's also hard to believe there are actually fish here.

The lower reaches of this stretch can be reached from near the Route 5 bridges. Five bridges have crossed the West Canada between Herkimer and East Herkimer over the years. From north to south they are: a wooden toll bridge, a cement arch bridge, the new Route 5 bridge that replaced the old Route 5 bridge (which was once a railroad bridge), and the still-standing stone-arch trolley bridge. The pools near the remnants of these bridges hold fish, especially in the spring of the year.

There are a number of pools between the Route 5 bridges and the mouth of the river, including those under the railroad bridge. They, and the mouth of the river, can be good bass and walleye water. Well-worn footpaths follow the riverbank in this area. A few successful walleye anglers drift worms in the pool where the West Canada meets the Mohawk.

WHAT'S HOT, WHAT'S NOT

The West Canada is an ever-changing river. Water high and cold, or low and warm. Fish on the prowl or hiding out. The lure, fly or bait that worked one day doesn't turn a fish the next. The best way to discover what's going on is to spend some time on the river. Second best is to talk to some of the people who make it their business to know what's going on.

The **West Canada Sport Shop,** on the west side of the bridge in Middleville, has been in operation since 1953. Hank Dimitri and Buck Flansburg have been telling fishermen what's happening on the river for years. And they sell the tackle, lures and bait you'll need to catch fish. Phone: 315-891-3804.

The **Golden Drake Fly Shop** is also in Middleville on Route 28. Randy Kulig has fly fished the West Canada for more than 20 years and shares his knowledge of the river from one of the most complete fly fishing shops in this part of the state. In addition to selling flies, fly tying materials and tackle, he teaches fly fishing and fly-tying at his shop and at Herkimer County Community College. Phone:315-891-3591.

Chapter 4
WILD COUNTRY
WILD TROUT

UPPER RIVER AIN'T WHAT IT USED TO BE
There was a time when West Canada Creek above Trenton Falls was a renowned brook trout fishery. Fishermen came here from the lower valley and from around New York State to catch speckled trout by the pack basket full. Those days are gone, but this area still offers opportunities for some exciting fishing.

SOURCE LAKES—BOUNCING BACK
The waters of West Lake, South Lake and Mud Lake become West Canada Creek at the outlet of Mud Lake. West Lake is the deepest and the most famous. In addition to being the only lake of the three that supported a healthy population of brook trout *and* lake trout for many years, this was also "Adirondack French Louie's" wilderness home at the turn of the century. And, until 1972 when this region of the Adirondacks was designated the West Canada Lakes Wilderness Area, this was the site of a New York State Ranger's Cabin. Today, backpackers stop here to see French Louie's stone fireplace, and sit on the rock foundation of the ranger cabin to enjoy the beauty of West Lake.

In Louie's time access was by lumber company roads and foot trails, so only the hardy made the long trek to fish the lakes and river, so there was plenty of fish for all. By the 1930s float planes were bringing anglers to these waters in increasing numbers, depleting the trout populations to such a degree aggressive stocking programs were instituted. Stocking continued into the 1960s, and although 16-inch brook trout and 5-pound lakers were caught as late as 1969, this fishery was deteriorating. By the mid 70s, increased water acidity had depleted populations of trout in many lakes and in the river. About this same time access was restricted to hikers only—no fly-ins, no vehicles. Stocking was terminated.

In the late 1980s, reports of angler success in some of the water-shed lakes, especially in the spring, sparked a new interest in this al-most forgotten fishery. Subsequent studies indicated reduced acidity and increased brook trout populations in many waters. In the 1990s stocking resumed in South Lake, plus such watershed lakes as Bear, Metcalf, Poor and Beaverdam Pond.

Today a few hardy anglers hike the 16-mile trail from Piseco Lake or the 10-mile trail from the Moose River Plains Recreation Area to fish the West Canada Lakes. Thus far the most productive fishery is the outlet of Mud Lake in the spring of the year. While Mud Lake has long been recognized as too shallow to support brook trout in the heat of summer, its warming spring waters and spawning suckers have al-ways attracted fish from the other lakes and from the river.

If subsequent studies determine that West Lake is not still "too acid", it will also be stocked with brook trout. Perhaps, as it was in French Louie's day, a few hardy fishermen will once again catch trout in all three lakes.

A FEW AND FAR BETWEEN FISHERY

Under ideal conditions—lots of cool, oxygenated water—brook trout , from the source to Nobleboro, are spread the length of the river. Catching them in this wild country is pretty much a hit and miss proposition, requiring miles of walking and hours of fishing to catch a few fish. There are times, however, when these spread-out fish come together. Generally, this concentration occurs twice a year. In the spring brook trout are attracted to sun-warmed stillwaters and rain-warmed tributaries. In late summer when most of the river is too warm and too low to support trout, they seek the cool, oxygen-rich waters of spring-holes, lake outlets, pools below waterfalls and cold-water tributaries.

There aren't many of these places on the upper West Canada, so knowing where they are and when the fish are there, are the keys to fishing this few and far between fishery. Unfortunately, the two major stillwaters on the river are on private land, so except for members of the Adirondack League Club, that leaves the mouths and lower-pools of tributary streams as the best places to fish for brook trout in the spring and late summer. Most of the tributary streams are noted in the "Fishing The Tribs" chapter, however, even the tiniest stream running into the river can attract brookies, especially in the spring, so it's a good idea to give them a try when you're in the area. Don't expect to catch big fish here—9-inchers are good size fish, and a 12-incher a real trophy.

Access to this part of the river from the south, starts on a few miles of well-maintained dirt road just north of Nobleboro; changes to a rutted, rocky road for more than a dozen miles, and ends with foot trails or compass headings through the woods. Access from the north is only by foot trails and compass headings. So, getting there is not easy, and for many trout fishermen, not worth the effort.

Where are the spring holes and waterfalls? Heh, part of the fun of fishing wilderness waters is discovery.

NOBLEBORO TO HINCKLEY LAKE
A HOT AND COLD FISHERY

DEC stocks brook trout in the river from Nobleboro to Wilmurt Falls and there's some natural production in tributary streams. Nevertheless, this too is a few and far between fishery, except right after the stocking truck leaves and when fish concentrate in the spring and summer. Like most of the upper river, spring holes and stream outlets are the best places to fish.

The stretch of river from the Wilmurt Falls to Hinckley Lake is stocked with both brookies and browns. Although some of these fish stay in river spring-holes or move into cold-water tribs during the summer, most of them drop down to the cooler waters of Hinckley Lake. The best time to catch them is in the spring when they come out of the lake, unless of course you take the time to locate the spring holes during the summer.

Access to this area is off Route 365 and Route 8. Much of this area is posted. Refer to map panels for location of state and private lands.

HINCKLEY LAKE AND PROSPECT POND
A WORLD OF DIFFERENCE

Hinckley Lake has exasperated fishermen for more than 70 years. Its waters are clean and cold just like a trout lake should be. The missing ingredient is fertility. The few nutrients that enter the lake from the river, feeder streams and shoreline runoff are flushed away at least once a year (sometimes twice) to control flooding and provide water for the Barge Canal, City of Utica, and power dams. *(See also Chapter 2)*

The best places to catch fish from Hinckley are at the mouths of feeder streams in the spring and, on rare occasions, in the heat of summer.

Prospect Pond (Lower Hinckley Lake) is a much different body of water than the big lake. Although water levels rise each night and fall each morning in response to the needs of the power plant near Prospect, water fluctuation is minimal compared to Hinckley. The bottom strata is also different, including gravel, sandy loam soils, and the beginning of limestone deposits (excellent acid buffers). This is also an area bordered by farm soils, providing nutrient rich runoff for the pond and river.

The result is that Prospect Pond is much more fertile than Hinckley Lake, and because it's just downstream from the big lake it's waters are always cold. Ideal trout water. Brown trout and rainbow trout are stocked in here, and they grow to enormous size. A few years back a 13-pound brown was caught just below Hinckley Dam, and local anglers catch a number of 20-inchers in this area every year. (See also Chapter 2)

While most of the big fish are caught in the stretch of water between the dam and the bridge at Hinckley, many other areas of the pond offer good opportunities to catch fish. This fishery is so new, few anglers have even tried to find the best places to take trout from other areas of the lake.

Some anglers ignore trout and spend their time catching bullheads, perch, rockbass and fallfish. The biggest fallfish I ever saw—a 2-1/2-pounder—came from Prospect Pond.

Access to this fishery is off Route 365. Fishing from shore is permitted upstream from the bridge at Hinckley and downstream on the village-side of the pond. There is additional shoreline access along Route 365 at the Prospect end. A small-boat launch is at the end near Prospect and a hand-launch near the bridge at Hinckley. Outboard motors, 10 hp or less are permitted.

TRENTON GORGE AND FALLS —NO MAN'S LAND

From the dam at Prospect Pond all the way to the dam at the village of Trenton Falls, West Canada Creek is posted, most of it by the Niagara Mohawk Power Corporation. Before you get upset about this big corporation restricting public access to their property on the river,

These three Adirondack Mountain lakes are the source of the West Canada. The only way to get to them is to hike 10 miles from Moose River Plains or 16 miles from Piseco Lake.

consider the fact that practically every year someone gets hurt or killed here. Falling down the side of the gorge or diving into the river below the falls and hitting underwater ledges, caused most of these accidents. Despite the fact that this area is heavily posted, most of these accidents result in lawsuits. One individual who fell into the gorge even sued the volunteer fire company that rescued her.

Because this area is posted, no fish are stocked here; natural production is nonexistent, and the water fluctuates so dramatically this stretch of the river is not good fishing and can be very dangerous to wade.

This is, however, the most beautiful stretch of the river, featuring a series of spectacular waterfalls that were once a world-famous tourist attraction. Efforts are underway to provide viewing access to the falls through a cooperative effort sponsored by the Town of Trenton and Niagara Mohawk.

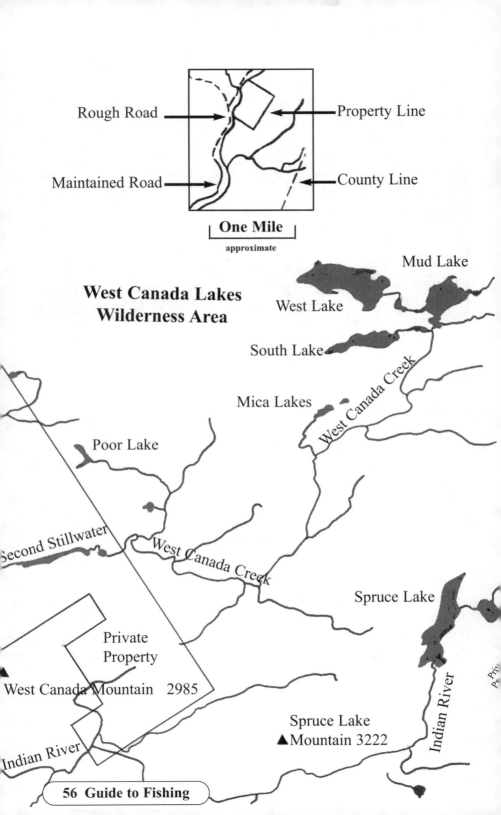

Rough Road ⟶ ⟵ Property Line

Maintained Road ⟶ ⟵ County Line

One Mile
approximate

Mud Lake

**West Canada Lakes
Wilderness Area**

West Lake

South Lake

Mica Lakes

West Canada Creek

Poor Lake

Second Stillwater

West Canada Creek

Spruce Lake

Private
Property

West Canada Mountain 2985

Spruce Lake
▲Mountain 3222

Indian River

Indian River

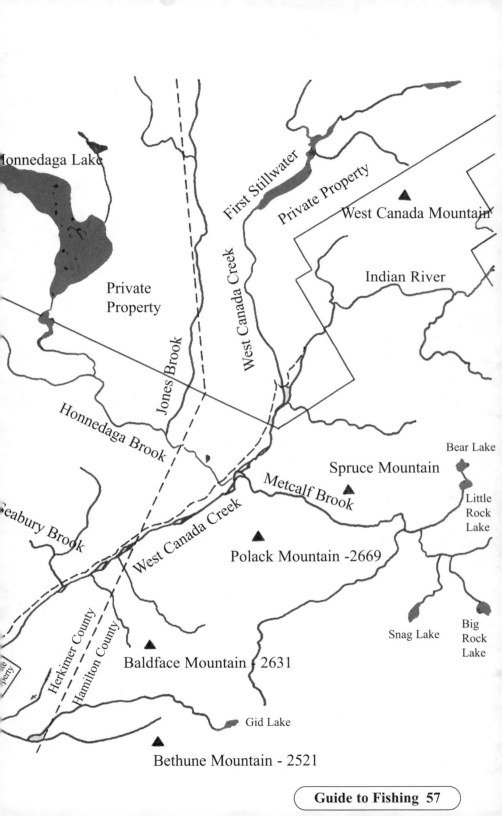

Honnedaga Lake

First Stillwater

Private Property

West Canada Mountain

Indian River

Private
Property

West Canada Creek

Jones Brook

Honnedaga Brook

Bear Lake

Spruce Mountain

Little
Rock
Lake

Metcalf Brook

Seabury Brook

West Canada Creek

Polack Mountain -2669

Herkimer County

Hamilton County

Snag Lake

Big
Rock
Lake

Baldface Mountain - 2631

Gid Lake

Bethune Mountain - 2521

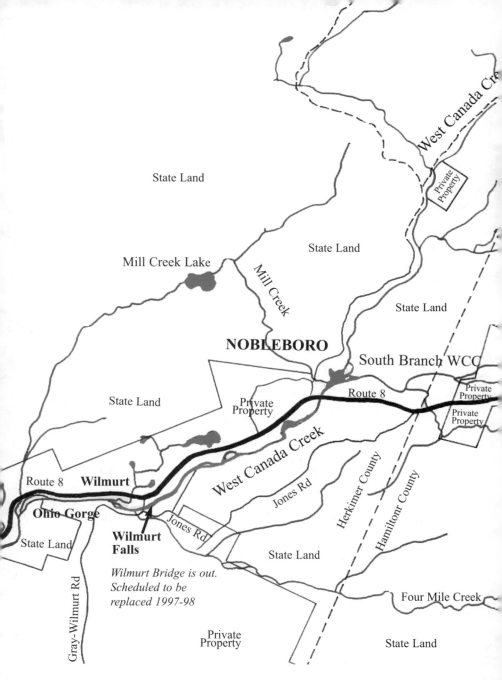

Wilmurt Falls protects the upstream brook trout fishery.
Although brown trout, rainbow trout, fallfish, perch and pickerel
have been introduced in the downstream river, streams and lake ,
these fish can't get over the falls at Wilmurt. This barrier has long
protected the fragile upstream brook trout fishery.

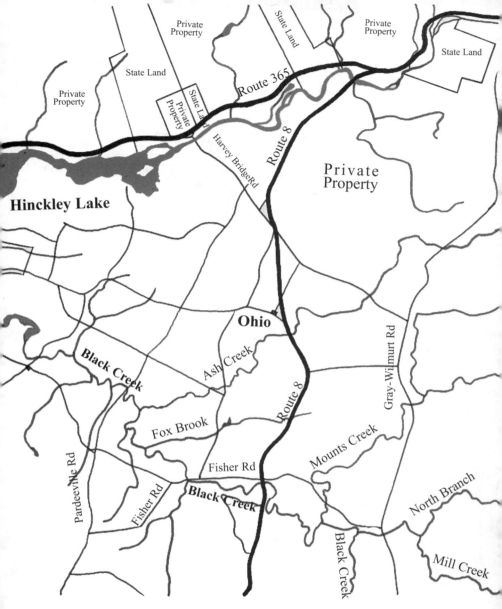

Natural Brook Trout Water

Beginning in the 1930s Black Creek and its many tributaries were heavily stocked with brook trout and rainbow trout. As more and more streamside lands were posted, stocking was reduced over the years, and eventually discontinued. Today these streams are natural brook trout waters. While access continues to be a problem in some areas, many stretches of these streams can be fished. Black Creek from Route 8 to Grant is a good stretch of water to canoe-fish. Look for the fallfish stone-pile nests in these streams.

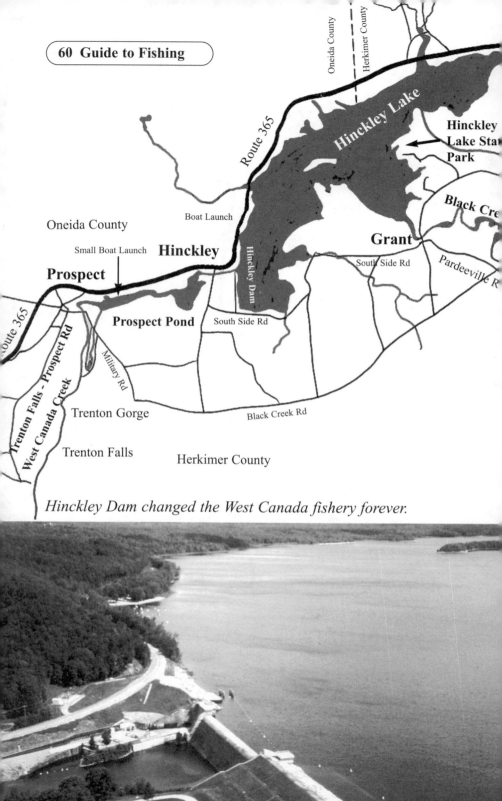

Route 365

Oneida County

Herkimer County

Hinckley Lake

Hinckley Lake State Park

Black Cre

Boat Launch

Oneida County

Small Boat Launch

Hinckley

Prospect

Grant

South Side Rd

Pardeeville R

Hinckley Dam

Prospect Pond

South Side Rd

Route 365

Trenton Falls - Prospect Rd

Military Rd

West Canada Creek

Trenton Gorge

Black Creek Rd

Trenton Falls

Herkimer County

Hinckley Dam changed the West Canada fishery forever.

SOUTH BRANCH
WEST CANADA CREEK

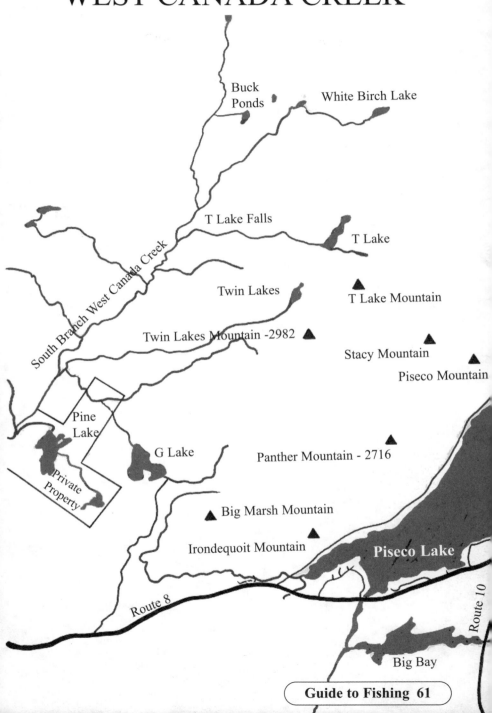

Buck
Ponds

White Birch Lake

T Lake Falls

T Lake

South Branch West Canada Creek

Twin Lakes

T Lake Mountain

Twin Lakes Mountain -2982

Stacy Mountain

Piseco Mountain

Pine
Lake

G Lake

Panther Mountain - 2716

Private
Property

Big Marsh Mountain

Irondequoit Mountain

Piseco Lake

Route 8

Route 10

Big Bay

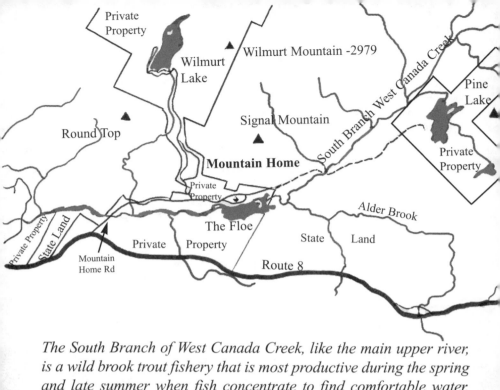

The South Branch of West Canada Creek, like the main upper river, is a wild brook trout fishery that is most productive during the spring and late summer when fish concentrate to find comfortable water. While most of the river runs through state land, most of the land around the The Floe at Mountain Home is privately owned.

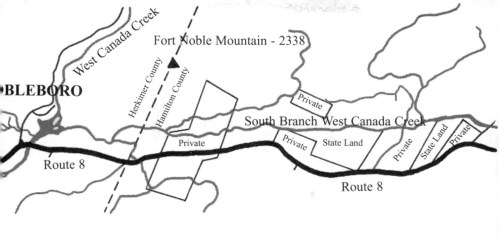

West Canada Creek

Fort Noble Mountain - 2338

BLEBORO

Herkimer County

Hamilton County

Private

South Branch West Canada Creek

Private

Private

State Land

Private

State Land

Private

Route 8

Route 8

The Adirondack Mountain waters of West Canada Creek and the South Branch of West Canada Creek meet at Nobleboro.

Chapter 5
FISHING THE TRIBS

West Canada Creek below Trenton Falls is without a doubt one of the most productive fisheries in New York State. If you like to fish big water and catch big fish, the lower river is the place to go. However, if small streams, wild trout and wild places turn you on, nothing compares to fishing the tribs'.

I've waded or canoed most of the tributaries below Trenton Falls, and a few streams in the upper valley. I've also talked to fishermen who fished them from the 1940s through the 90s. And I've read the memoirs of fishermen who fished them in the late 1800s and early 1900s.

Like the West Canada, this has been an up and down fishery. In the late 1700s every one of these streams was brook trout water. After settlement the lower-valley streams were starved of water and polluted by mills in the villages. In the late 1800s when the mills moved to the main river, brook trout returned to some waters, and in the early 1900s they were stocked with brookies, rainbows or browns. Today, except for Cincinnati Creek, none of them are stocked with fish. Wild brook trout have returned in many of these streams, supplemented by brown trout that come up from the river.

Much of the information I discovered about fishing in this area at the turn of the century came from the unpublished **"Reminiscences of Sherman O. Klock"** This wealth of information included many references to fishing such streams as Wolf Hollow Brook, Black Creek, upper West Canada, Jock's Lake (Honondega) Outlet, Metcalf Creek and Indian River. Sherman fished these streams using worms, beetles, grasshoppers, wet flies and dry flies, and caught thousands of brook trout. In the smaller streams he caught 7–10 inch fish, and an occasional 12-incher. In bigger water he caught 1–2 pound fish, and an occasional 3-pounder. On the smallest tribs he often crawled to the streambank so he didn't spook fish.

Much of the information I discovered about fish in the tributaries during the 1930s came from the New York State **1934 Biological Survey** of the West Canada watershed. The survey report included the names, locations, stocking levels and quality of water on almost every stream (and lake) in the watershed. (See Chapter 2)

CHANCE MEETING FILLS IN THE GAP

When I first started my quest to wade, canoe and fish all the tributaries in the lower valley, I had the good fortune to stop for a late lunch at the Main Street Ristorante in Newport. There were no other customers when I walked in the door—half-way between lunch and dinner—so I chose a table close to the counter. As I devoured a bowl of Manhattan clam chowder, a small loaf of wheat bread and three cups of coffee, I chatted with Kim (Assaro)and Ryan De Faria.

While I talked to the owners, chief cooks and dish washers (except for some help from relatives, they do it all) Bill Shumway walked in the door for his afternoon coffee. Bill had come to this area from the Adirondack Mountains in the 1940s where he had fished such famous streams as the Ausable and Saranac rivers. It didn't take long for him to discover the trout in the West Canada and its tributaries. I learned that Bill had fished many of the West Canada tribs' in the 50s through the 70s, and still fly-fishes the river near his home in Newport. I had discovered a source of information that filled the gap between the 1930s and 70s.

From that day on, I planned my Thursday outings so I could stop for lunch around 2.pm. Kim and Ryan always made a point to ask me what stream I had visited that day and patiently listened while I told them about my adventure and the historical significance of the area. When Bill came for coffee, I told him about the fish I had caught and lost . . . and we talked fish and fishing.

After one of these conversations, I asked Bill if he would show me some of the West Canada streams he had fished over the years. We spent a half day driving the back roads and reliving some of Bill's experiences on such streams as Shed Brook, Wolf Hollow, Hurricane, Four Mile and the South Branch.

While Bill is primarily a fly fisherman, he seldom cast flies to tributary fish because there was "no room to cast a fly". A *gold* willow-leaf spinner with *red* beads and a worm at the end of short, light spinning outfit took most of the brookies and browns he caught.

Other West Canada anglers, like longtime friend Ron Gugnacki, who had fished the tribs' in the 70 and 80s, used worms to take browns from such streams as Mill Creek, Terry Brook and Cincinnati

Creek. When the water was clear he caught small fish, but when it was dirty just after a rainstorm he caught 12–14-inch fish.

LOWER RIVER TRIBS HAVE MUCH IN COMMON

Practically every Thursday in the spring and summer of 1996, I waded or canoed one of the tribs'. Although I carried a spinning rod, my primary interest at the time was gathering information and photos for my book on West Canada Valley. I seldom came prepared with bait or a variety of lures. For the most part, I cast a small gold Phoebe because it's a good lure in shallow water and West Canada trout seem to like it. In some streams, like Old City (Wolf Hollow) Brook , I didn't raise a fish, but in most streams I caught browns, brookies, fallfish and chubs.

All of these streams pass through private land. While walking up from the mouth, I saw very few posted signs, and no one asked me to leave. On many of these streams, the upstream, easy-access areas are posted.

In the lower valley, I soon discovered that every stream but one has a limestone waterfall or series of waterfalls that trout can't get over. The pools and runs below these waterfalls are excellent places to find concentrations of fish that come up from the main river. When the big river is cold and dirty during the spring runoff, trout move into these warmer, cleaner waters. I discovered some nice browns, plus some big suckers and fallfish below the falls in the spring. During the summer and fall, the deeper pools in these same areas produced browns up to 12 inches, plus some chubs.

Here's a brief rundown on the streams I hiked or canoed in 1996. I started at the mouth and waded upstream two to four hours. The two streams I canoed, I took out at or near the mouth of the stream. Refer to the map panels for location.

NORTH CREEK (the southernmost tributary)—June 27—started at the mouth of the creek where I discovered low water and poor fishing conditions. If I had come to fish, I would have left. Two miles up, caught three browns (9—11 inches) and had many hits below a waterfalls at the site of an old mill dam. Wildlife—owl, green heron, kingfisher, sandpiper and song birds. Lots and lots of minnows.

STONY CREEK—September 19—isolated water, not easy to get to mouth of stream. Some excellent looking pools just up from mouth

There are waterfalls on every tributary but one in the lower valley.

and below waterfalls. Water dirty below waterfalls; cows walking in the water upstream. Caught chubs, saw suckers and lots of minnows. Wildlife—great blue heron, ducks, songbirds. Got to go back in the spring.

MALTANNER CREEK—April 25—caught two 12-inch browns from a pool created by a fallen log in the woods above Middleville. Further up, the pool below the waterfalls called Cupid's Retreat, looked great but no fish. Found two empty worm containers beside the pool.

OLD CITY (WOLF HOLLOW) BROOK—April 18 and August 20—limestone bed starts just above the mouth of the brook and significant waterfalls start a half-mile upstream. Several waterfalls on this stream, with high waterfalls just above and below "Old City". This area was the site of the first mills in West Canada Valley (1790) above Herkimer. No fish caught. August trip—wildflowers and minnows. . Sherman Klock and Bill Shumway caught trout in the slow waters well upstream from the falls.

WHITE CREEK—August 15—water low and warm. Great looking pools just up from Route 28. Had caught small browns here in the spring, but no trout on this trip, just a few chubs. Good pools below waterfalls at old mill site a couple of miles upstream. Wildlife—kingfisher, hawk, songbirds. Wildflowers. Hurricane Brook is a tributary of this stream and Bill Shumway caught brook trout here.

SHED BROOK—May 2—some nice holes and runs from the mouth to the first waterfalls, just a half-mile upstream. Big hole at the bottom of the lower falls. Caught a huge sucker on a worm, no trout. Bill Shumway caught some nice browns here on flies. Beautiful series of waterfalls.

TERRY BROOK—August 19—the only stream I found in the lower valley that does not feature a waterfalls. Runs through a steep-sided, wooded valley. Water was cool, but didn't raise a fish. Wildlife—lots of deer tracks. Wild flowers. Ron Gugnacki caught browns here in the spring.

COLD BROOK—July 26—a well-named stream. Dramatic difference in water temperature when wading with sneakers from West Canada into mouth of brook. Except for a few casts into the river near the mouth, didn't fish until above the Kuyahoora Valley Park. From there to the falls in the village of Cold Brook caught several nice brook trout, the biggest 12 inches. This stream was once lined with mills that restricted waterflow and polluted the stream. The natural production of brook trout in recent years is an excellent example of what happens when cold water is cleaned up. Catch and release is the only way to maintain this fragile fishery. Wildflowers.

MILL CREEK—August 1—water cool but low. Good looking holes and runs from the mouth to Route 28, and a mile or so upstream from the Route 28 bridge. No fish caught, although had caught browns here in the spring in previous years. Good looking pools below the falls in Gravesville. A youngster was fishing with worms, hadn't caught anything, but did well earlier in the week. This section was too polluted for stocking in the 1930s. Wildflowers. Ron Gugnacki caught many browns from this stream in the spring.

CINCINNATI CREEK—June 13—after two days of rain; paddled, carried and dragged a one man canoe from the Route 28 bridge near Mapledale to the mouth of the creek and down to the first takeout on

The tribs are good places to fish when the river is high. This fat brown was taken from a log-hole in Maltanner Creek in April.

the West Canada. Many fallen trees blocked the creek. Caught three brown trout; many follows and hits on a gold Phoebe. Landed a 12-inch brookie that ate a tiny crayfish plug. Wildlife—mallards, wood ducks, mergansers. Wildflowers. Great adventure!

This is the most historically significant tributary of West Canada Creek and one of the best brown trout streams in the area. General Baron Von Steuben traveled this stream by canoe and bateaux to get to his holdings in the early 1800s. Brook trout teemed here until mills in Barneveld and Remsen restricted and polluted the water. By the 1890s this stream and its tributary, Steuben Creek, were cleaned up enough to stock trout. From then until now the Cincinnati has been stocked with brown trout. Stocking levels were reduced considerably in recent years because so much land along the stream was posted. Cool water running over nutrient rich farm soils, limestone rock and gravel bottom—plus some domestic pollution—make this the only recognized natural-production brown trout water in the valley. The first major falls on the Cincinnati is upstream from Barneveld.

UPPER VALLEY TRIBS—A FEAST OR FAMINE FISHERY

From the source-lakes to Hinckley Lake, brook trout reign, but their numbers are limited by the scarcity of cold, deep water in the heat of summer, by lack of nutrients, and to some degree by the continuing effects of acid precipitation. Most of the time these fish are spread out along the river and tribs, so catching them is a hit and miss proposition. However, when fish are seeking warm water in the spring, and cold water in the summer, many of these tributaries attract concentrations of fish. Most of them are caught on worms, spinner and worm, spinners and spoons. A few are caught on brook trout flies.

Most of these streams are not easy to get to. Access areas are often posted, located on back country roads or at the end of hiking trails. See map panels for location of streams, private lands, state lands and roads. A topographical map of the area will provide information on hiking trails.

BLACK CREEK—July 6 (not a Thursday) my wife Gert and I canoed from the Route 8 bridge to Grant. A half-mile downstream talked to two bank-fishermen who caught a few small brookies on worms. A number of small brook trout followed my Phoebe but wouldn't take it. Wildlife—mallards, mergansers, great blue heron, kingfisher. Wildlflowers.

I have canoed and fished this stream a number of times over the years and never got into fish, although I know that both brook trout and fallfish spawn here. The fallfish nests are fascinating. These piles of pebbles and rocks up to three feet high and six feet long can be seen in the creek during low water periods.

Sherman Klock caught some big brookies here in the late 1800s near mill dams. Black Creek and its many tributaries were heavily stocked with trout in the mid 1900s. (See Chapter 2) Stocking was decreased and eventually stopped as more and more access areas were posted. Local anglers in the know take good catches of brookies on worms, lures and flies from the Black and its tribs.

THE FOUR MILE—Bill Shumway caught brook trout here, but stopped fishing it because of posting just upstream from the mouth. Most of this stream is on state land, but requires a hike to get to it. Brook trout still spawn here.

SOUTH BRANCH—(South Branch West Canada Creek) Good to excellent fishing for brook trout in spring holes, near stream and lake outlets during the late summer months. Considerable private and posted land in the lower reaches. Sherman Klock caught brookies here by the basket full. Bill Shumway didn't do that well, but took some good brookies from stillwaters.

HONONDEGA BROOK—The Haskell family has had a camp in this area since 1908, and recorded their fishing success in the Camp Guest Book since the 1940s. The size and number of fish caught has been up and down over the years, but most of their good catches on this stream were made in late July and August when brookies were seeking cold water. Sherman Klock fished here before and after Trume Haskell built his camp, and caught many "pounds" of fish in the early 1900s.

METCALF BROOK—another Haskell Camp water that has produced good catches of trout when they were concentrated in cold water areas during the summer months. Klock also notes the pools and lake outlets along this stream were teeming with trout in the late 1800s and early 1900s.

INDIAN RIVER—Sherman Klock visited lumber camps, and camped and fished in this area where he caught brook trout by the pack basket full. Not that many fish here today, but still productive brook trout water at spring holes and cold stream outlets. Seldom fished because its not easy to get to.

Chapter 6
FISH
TO
CATCH

The primary sportfish in the West Canada and its tributaries are trout. Brook trout dominate the fishery in the upper valley, and are found in most watershed lakes and tributaries as well as in the river. This is primarily a wild trout fishery, although brookies are stocked in the Nobleboro area and in some watershed lakes. Brookies and browns are stocked from Wilmurt Falls to Hinckley Dam; browns and rainbows in Prospect Pond.

Brown trout dominate the lower river fishery, although brook trout and smallmouth bass are also present. Brown trout are the only fish stocked in this area.

Fallfish are found throughout the river system from Wilmurt Falls to Herkimer, and walleyes are present near the mouth of the river.

Knowing something about the habits of these fish can improve fishing success. Knowing how to identify different species can be part of the fun of fishing, and help to avoid taking fish out of season.

TROUT
Trout have a small dorsal fin just ahead of the tail (adipose fin), **no** barbels around the mouth, tiny soft scales, and spots on the darker colored parts of their body. Most of the spots are black or brown, but the more striking spots feature such colors as red, orange and blue.

BROOK TROUT
New York's official state fish and only native stream trout. Prefers clean, cold, well oxygenated water. Preferred temperatures are 57—61 degrees F. Spawns in the fall, October—December, in tributary streams with a good gravel bottom. Preferred foods are insects (larva and adult), crayfish, small fish, and worms that wash into streams.

Brook trout feature red spots surrounded by a blue ring. Bottom fins are orange to pink. Average size 8–10 inches, up to 16 inches; 2 pounds.

BROWN TROUT
Came to New York from Europe in 1883; stocked in some West Canada tribs as early as 1897. Prefers clean, moderately flowing water. Tolerates warmer water and more pollution than brook trout. Preferred temperatures 54–64 degrees F. Spawns in the fall, October–November, in streams with good gravel bottom. Preferred foods are insects (larva and adult), crayfish, small fish and worms that wash into streams.

Brown trout feature large orange and red spots. Belly is creamy white. Average size 10–12 inches, up to 28 inches; 8+ pounds.

RAINBOW TROUT
Came to New York from the west coast in 1874; stocked in some West Canada tribs and lakes in the early 1900's. Prefers fast-flowing, turbulent streams. Can tolerate water temperatures up to 80 degrees F.,higher than any other New York trout. Preferred temperatures 57–60 degrees F. Spawns in the **spring**, March—April, in streams with good gravel bottom. Preferred foods are insects (larva and adult) fish eggs and small fish.

Rainbow trout feature many small dark spots and pink to red "rainbow" sides. Belly is white to silver. Average size 10–12 inches, up to 20 inches; 3 pounds.

BASS
Bass are of the sunfish family, but are longer and larger than most of their cousins. Like all sunfish they have a spiny dorsal fin and hard scales.

SMALLMOUTH BASS
A native fish that reproduces naturally in the lower river. Prefers moderate to fast water near rocks. Preferred temperatures 65–75 degrees F. Spawns in spring, May—June, over gravel or rocky bottom. Preferred foods are insects (larva and adult), crayfish and small fish.

Smallmouth bass are brown to greenish brown and often feature vertical bars on sides. The back corner of the mouth is even with the eye. Average Size 10–14 inches, up to 18 inches; 3 pounds.

Note: Largemouth bass are not common, however, they are occasionally caught. The largemouth has a green to black body with a dark horizontal band on sides from head to tail. The back corner of the mouth extends behind the eye— hence "largemouth".

FALLFISH
New York's largest native freshwater minnow. Prefers moderate to slow water with gravel to rocky bottom. Preferred temperatures are

unknown, but are active from late spring to early fall. Spawns in May on huge nests that the male fallfish builds by carrying rocks and pebbles in its mouth and piling them in mounds as large as six feet long and three feet high. Preferred foods are insects (larva and adult) crayfish, small fish and worms that wash into streams. Fallfish can save the day when trout and bass are not active.

Fallfish have an olive brown back and silvery sides, with barbels on its mouth. It does not have an adipose fin or spots on sides. Average Size: 9—12 inches, up to 18 inches; 2 pounds.

WALLEYE
A native fish that reproduces naturally near the mouth of the river. Prefers moderate flowing, clean but cloudy water with sand and gravel bottom. Preferred temperatures 60—70 degrees. **Spawns in spring** on gravel bottom soon after ice out and water temperatures are 45–50 F. Preferred foods are fish, crayfish, insect larva and worms that wash into streams.

Walleye are grayish yellow to brownish (golden) yellow with dark bands or blotches on sides. Has **two dorsal fins and a forked tail that is white on the lower lobe**. Canine teeth in lower jaw, and large "glassy" eyes. Average size: 15–18 inches, up to 20 inches; 3 pounds.

FISHING SEASON AND LIMITS

Fishing seasons and limits change from time to time, so a review of the current New York State Fishing Regulations Guide is suggested.

Trout

April 1–October 15
Source-lakes to Trenton Falls—5 fish, any size; lures and bait.
(*No baitfish allowed in the West Canada Lakes Wilderness Area.*)

April 1–November 30
Trenton Falls to the mouth of Cincinnati Creek Special Waters Section—artificial Lures only 3 fish, 12 inches *until Oct 97.*

Starting in October 1997 this Special Waters Section becomes a No Kill Section—artificial lures only.

April 1—November 30
Mouth of Cincinnati Creek to mouth of river.
5 fish, any size; lures and bait.

Bass

Third Saturday in June- March 15
5 fish, 12 inches; lures and bait.

Fallfish—no closed season, no limits

Walleye

First Saturday in May—March 15
5 fish, 15 inches; lures and bait

Chapter 7
SPIN FISHING

Spin fishing is the most popular way to take fish on the West Canada. A spinning rod and reel, loaded with ultra smooth monofilament line, allows a fisherman to cast lures and bait great distances . . . and cover more water than any other method.

While there are valid arguments for long rods, short rods, ultra-light rods and medium-action rods—that work best for different fish under different conditions—a light-action 5-1/2- to 6-foot spinning outfit will handle most situations on the river and tributaries. Loaded with 6-pound test monofilament line, it will provide plenty of action even with a small fish at the end of the line, yet handle a heavy fish. For clear water, a change to 4-pound test will produce more fish, while 8-pound test is a good idea if you're after big fish and the water is cloudy or dirty.

Number 5, 7 and 10 snap swivels will connect line to lures. Number 4, 6 and 8 hooks will hold most bait, and an assortment of split-hot sinkers will take it down to fish.

A fishing vest is ideal for carrying tackle, but a belly pack will suffice. A pair of long nose-pliers and a net are a good idea, as is a wading staff if you plan to wade the river. Waders are best for the river; hip boots for the tribs in the colder months. Sneakers are good for warm-water wading.

LURES THAT CATCH FISH

You can fill many tackle boxes with the lures that will catch fish in the West Canada, but you don't need that many. Here's a good starter kit.

Phoebe (gold): More West Canada trout are caught on this minnow-shaped spoon than any other lure. It's especially good for shallow, clear water because it's not heavy and it flashes like crazy. It will usually take fish on a steady retrieve, but sometimes jerking the rod tip makes it work best.

Blue Fox Vibrax Spinner (gold)—good for deeper runs and cloudy water because it's heavy and it vibrates. Jerking the rod tip on retrieve sometimes makes it work better.

Floating Rapala Minnow (gold)—good for taking big trout anytime of year. Works best if Rapala knot is used to tie line to lure, and when the rod tip is jerked and reel speed varied on retrieve. Bigger lure, bigger fish.

Rebel Crawfish and Wee Crawfish (natural) —*big-lipped version*— good for taking trout and bass in rocky pools and runs where they normally feed on crayfish. Works best if it ticks the bottom on the retrieve.

Mepps Spinners (gold with red sleeve) good for trout and bass if retrieved while jerking the rod tip.

Plastic Jigs (yellow, white and chartreuse). are very effective bass and walleye lures. They look like a variety of fish foods, so a variety of retrieves are in order. Just swimming the jig with a few changes in reel speed can take fish. Jerking the rod tip up, retrieving slack line and then jerking again turns some fish on. Sometimes a slow lift instead of the jerk upward works best.

CAST ABOVE AND BEYOND

When fishing from shore or wading, cast diagonally upstream and slightly beyond where fish are holding. This allows the lure or bait time to sink before you work it by the fish's nose. In slower-moving water the same presentation takes fish, however, you also have the options of casting cross stream, downstream and directly upstream, depending on water depth and speed, and weight of lure or bait.

Some situations require special skills and techniques to present lures to feeding fish. For example a fish haven the size of a small bath tub, requires pinpoint accuracy and an immediate retrieve to get results. Getting a lure to the fish in a pile of logs or undercut bank, may require allowing the lure to drift downstream into this type of cover before retrieving it—much like fishing bait.

Many lures take fish on the West Canada, but here's a good starter selection: Top—Floating Rapala Minnow (gold). Bottom—left to right—Blue Fox Vibrax Spinner(gold), Phoebe (gold) and a Rebel Crawfish (natural).

HOW TO RIG AND FISH BAIT

Some bait fishermen hook a gob of worms on a big hook, weight it down with a half-ounce of sinker, cast it into a big hole and wait . . . and wait . . . and wait. Some of the biggest fish of the year are caught this way every year, usually early in the season.

Many more fish, however, are caught throughout the year by drifting or working baits that look like natural food. The most popular natural foods are worms, minnows and crayfish. Here's how to rig and fish them.

Start all three of these bait rigs with enough sinker to take the bait down to the fish and still let it look as natural as possible. That means as little weight as possible attached approximately 15 inches up the line from the hook. Trial, error and experience will determine how much weight works best at different depths and current flow.

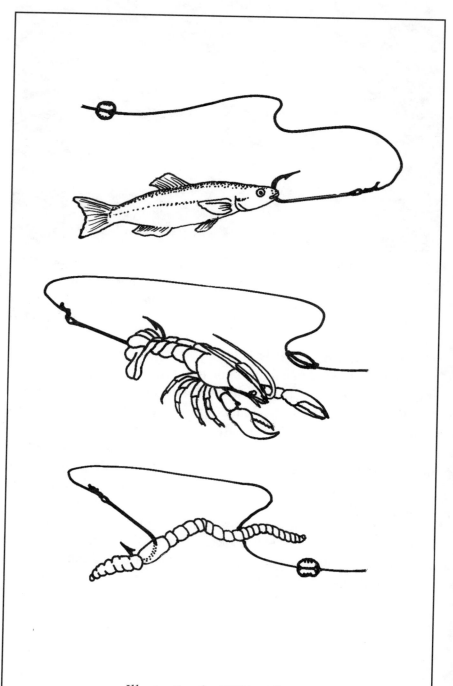

Illustration by William Davis

Hook a minnow up through the lips and fish it like a worm, or retrieve it with a slow twitching motion of the rod tip. In deeper, slow-moving water a minnow can be hooked through the back just ahead of the dorsal fin and fished below a bobber. A Size 6 hook is good for the smaller trout and bass minnows.

Hook a crayfish up through the tail, about three segments from the tip. After drifting the crayfish through fishy water, let it swing around in the current. Get ready for a hit. If you don't get a hit and the water is deep enough, work the bait toward you with a slow jerking motion. A Size 4 hook will do fine.

As with lures, presenting bait is not always as simple as casting, drifting and retrieving. Sometimes special techniques are required for special places. Some situations require hand-feeding the line as the bait drifts directly downstream into a hole or pool. When the bottom is so cluttered with rubble that it "eats" tackle, bait suspended from a small bobber or a float will take fish.

Hook a worm or nightcrawler (sometimes half a nightcrawler is plenty) through the middle or the breeding ring. Cast it above fish havens and let it sink to the bottom. Take in slack line, leaving a good bend, and allow the bait to drift downstream. When you feel a hit or see the line tighten or jump, set the hook. Remember, use just enough sinker to take the bait to the bottom. A Size 6 hook is good for most situations, but a Size 8 may take more fish in clear water.

WHERE THEY ARE AND WHAT THEY LIKE

TROUT are the most sought after fish in the West Canada. Except for rainbows, trout stay out of rapids, preferring instead to hold just out of fast water where meals are delivered by the current and minimum energy is required to stay in feeding position. Trout wait for food at the head and tail of pools; front and back of rocks, logs, bridge abutments, islands, along undercut banks and in long deep runs. Those slow-water pools below islands, large rocks and bridge abutments provide trout havens that can extend downstream for 50 yards or more.

During the summer months, anything that can offer cool water, oxygen and shade will attract trout, so coldwater springs, stream outlets, pools below rapids, riffles and waterfalls, and shoreline shade will concentrate fish.

Trout like spinners, spoons and plugs and small jigs that look like minnows, crayfish and insects. Browns like gold and yellow, brookies like a touch of red.

The best bait for brown and brook trout is a worm, with minnows and crayfish running a close second. Rainbow trout prefer minnows but will take worms.

SMALLMOUTH BASS like pools and eddies below rapids and waterfalls, small bays, quiet water at stream bends, rock piles, logs, stream outlets, islands, bridge abutments and dams.

Smallmouths like spinners, plugs and jigs that look like minnows, crayfish and insects.

The best bait for smallies is a crayfish. Second best is a minnow.

FALLFISH like the quiet waters of pools, holes, eddies and small bays, but will feed in fast water where they can stay out of the current behind rocks or other obstructions.

Most fallfish are caught by anglers seeking trout and bass, because they inhabit the same waters and hit many of the same lures and bait. They like flashy spoons and spinners. They love worms.

WALLEYE prefer the bottom of deep pools near piles of logs, rocks, bridge abutments, dams and stream outlets. In the evening and on cloudy days they often move out of the deep pools to feed in runs and near piles of debris.

They like jigs, spinners and plugs that look like insect larva, leeches and minnows. The best bait is a nightcrawler. Second best is a minnow. Slow moving lures and baits on the bottom work best.

UP AND DOWN WATER TURNS FISH ON AND OFF

Each day around 9 a.m. the power plants above Trenton Falls run water through their turbines to provide power to meet increased demands at the start of the day. While these turbines are on line, the water level in the river rises a foot or more, depending on the season, power demands and available water. This rush of water travels down the river about 5 mph, reaching Poland around noon and Herkimer in early evening. While this high water is a boon to floating the river, it can have a dramatic effect on fishing.

An hour or more after the water comes up, most West Canada fish are turned off. Insect activity comes to a halt, other food sources relocate, and water depth and current increase dramatically. The river environment changes so much it takes awhile for fish to adjust. Some anglers take a coffee break, others fish the tributaries, and a few fish the recently flooded shallow waters.

It's not difficult to work around the water fluctuation, and in some cases to benefit from it. There is plenty of time to fish the river before and after the water comes up. For instance the lower stretches (below Middleville) aren't affected until afternoon, and by noon the water is back down near Trenton Falls. By evening the entire river is usually at a lower level. Of course you can also fish below Trenton Falls in the early morning hours before the water release, but it can be very dangerous if you're in mid-stream when the water comes up.

Some anglers think it's worth the risk, because for 15-30 minutes before the water comes up—anywhere on the river— there is often a feeding frenzy. How the fish know high water is coming is a mystery.

STUDIES SHOW WHEN AND HOW TO CATCH FISH

Several studies were conducted on the West Canada over the years to determine when most people fished the river and which fishermen were the most successful. All of them indicated there were more fishermen on the river early in the season when fishing was poorest, and their numbers diminished as fishing improved later in the season. The most successful fishermen walked or waded the river; the least successful fished in one spot.

Chapter 8
FLY FISHING

West Canada Creek is known far and wide as one of the best fly fishing streams in the northeast. Fishermen travel from all over to cast flies to the brown trout that feed in its runs, riffs and pools. I've met many of these fishermen over the years; some of them novices, some experts, a few "professionals".

Three professional fly fishermen have helped shape my understanding and appreciation for the sport of casting bits of feather and hair for trout. Together they span almost 70 years of fly fishing West Canada Creek.

Jack McDiarmid came to this area from western New York in the early 1900s to work as a "dynamiter" on the construction of Hinckley Dam. He remained in the area and started fishing on "West Creek" in the 1920s.

For many years Jack taught fly fishing and fly tying at the New York State Conservation Camp at Lake Colby, at Conservation Education Days in Oneida County, and at sportsmen clubs. He also demonstrated his fly-casting skills, including casting with two rods at the same time, at area outdoor shows.

Among his many friends and acquaintances were such world-famous fly fishermen as Lee Wulff, Joe Brooks and H.G. Tapply. One of his most memorable experiences was the day he carried Joe Brooks off West Canada Creek. Joe had fallen and broken his leg.

Jack's favorite stretch of the river was between Hinckley and Prospect, now under Prospect Pond. He told of catching hundreds of brookies, browns and rainbows here in the '40s and '50s. On the lower river one of his special pools was just downstream from Cameron Covered Bridge. Jack fly fished this pool before and after the bridge was burned in the 1930s. When he was 87 years old he caught a 22-inch brown here.

I met Jack at the Trenton Fish and Game Club in the 1960s. Like almost everyone who met him, I instantly became his friend. He taught my late wife Janice how to tie flies and he taught me how to cast them. Janice was a much better student than I. She could tie feathers and hair on a Number 22 hook with ease. I managed to catch a few small trout in Cincinnati Creek, but much to Jack's disappointment, I never mastered the fly rod.

Jack tied hundreds of different flies and he could match the hatch with the best of them, but he emphasized that the real trick to catching fish on a fly was to know where the fish was, to approach it unseen and to present the fly so it looked like food in the water. To prove these points he often demonstrated catching big trout with his favorite fly—that represents nothing in particular—the Royal Coachman.

Jack was 97 years old when he passed away on February 9, 1985. I like to think he's still fishing West Canada Creek. To me, and hundreds of others, he will always be Mr. West Canada Creek.

John Bianco's first experience on the West Canada was rolling into it as an infant. Before he could become fishfood, his father, Felix yanked him out of the river so he could rejoin the family picnic/ fishing outing.

John's father loved West Canada Creek and fished it as a "walking bait fisherman" three times a week for many years. John joined him on many of these outings and from time to time saw fly fishermen on the river. In the early '50s when John was 15 his father bought him a fly rod. At first he used it to catch trout with worms, later with a few flies he bought at the old Horrick Ibbotson (HI) Store in Utica. He didn't know any fly fishermen and was too shy to talk to those he met on the river, so he started reading everything he could about flies and fly fishing.

In the early 70s he joined Trout Unlimited, attended TU conventions and talked to such fly fishing gurus as Art Flick and Francis Betters. John became engrossed in identifying insects, spouting their Latin names and matching the hatch. He traveled throughout the state and to faraway places to catch fish on flies and learn more about fly fishing. When he was home he fished the West Canada almost every day of the week.

He shared his knowledge and skills at TU meetings, outdoor shows and fish and game clubs. For a time he owned a fly fishing shop in New York Mills where he taught fly fishing and fly tying, and made fly rods. Today he still sells custom fly rods and teaches fly fishing at Mohawk Valley Community College.

I met John in the early 70s and we've been friends ever since. I've watched him evolve from a good fly fisherman, who could rattle off Latin names of watery insects, to become a master fly fisherman who spends less time matching the hatch and more time seeking a few big fish.

John still fishes the West Canada almost every evening of the season, casting one of a handful of flies that consistently take fish. One of his favorite runs is downstream from the end of Putnam Road. His favorite fly for fishing fast water is the "Haystack", a fly developed by Francis Betters for the Ausable River. John caught and released a 28-inch brown, estimated to weigh 8 pounds, on one of these flies from some "heavy water" below Poland in the fall of 1995.

I fished with John on the West Canada recently. He emphasized locating the spots where fish lie, approaching with care, and presenting the fly so it drifts by the fish looking like something to eat. Sound familiar?

Side by side we waded a stretch of heavy water, alternating casting with John's fly rod. He's right-handed and I'm a lefty, so this method of demonstration and instruction worked perfectly.

"Look at the way the currents cross behind those rocks. That's where the best fish lie. Cast above that spot. In this heavy water a Haystack will stay on the surface without dressing. It doesn't have to look exactly like a natural fly because the current is moving so fast a fish doesn't have time to study it.

"When drifting a fly on pools or slow runs, a more natural looking fly works best, and don't be afraid to give that fly a twitch or jiggle once in awhile. A horizontal shake of the rod tip will do it."

I learned a lot that afternoon, and even managed to catch my first West Canada brown trout on a fly. Jack would have been proud.

Randy Kulig started fly fishing when he was 15 years old. He read everything he could find about fly fishing and fly tying, joined Trout Unlimited, picked the brains of experts, and traveled far and wide to catch fish and learn more about catching them on artificial critters made from feathers, hair and synthetic materials.

He first cast a fly in the West Canada in the early '70s. Fly fishing the West Canada became such an obsession he and his family moved from Fort Plain to Middleville. Five years ago he and wife Carol opened the Golden Drake Fly Shop. Today he teaches fly tying and fly fishing at his shop and at Herkimer County Community College, and demonstrates his skills and knowledge at outdoor shows.

While Randy and his customers and students fish the entire lower river, he is especially knowledgeable about the waters between Poland and Herkimer, including the relatively new trout water below Middleville. We talked about these fish-havens for hours, discussing such topics as access areas, names of pools and runs, numbers and sizes of fish, best lies and what flies work best.

In response to questions he has heard time and time again, Randy offered the following.

Where are the best places to catch fish?

"You can catch fish just about everywhere in the West Canada, but this is not an easy river to fish everywhere. It's a big river and difficult to wade in most areas because of the heavy current and all the round rocks on the bottom. In some areas where the water looks flat, the bottom is not; there are depression (holes) in the bottom that drop a couple of feet. (A real surprise when you're up to your waist in midstream.)

"There are plenty of stocked fish in the areas close to the roads where most people fish, and there are big browns, some very big browns, in places away from the roads.

"Wherever you fish, keep in mind that trout have three basic requirements: shelter from current . . . protection from above . . . and food.

"Shelters from the current are in such places as pools and holes, behind (and directly in front of) rocks and logs.

"Protection from above—where most predators come from — is under logs, rocks, overhanging trees, undercut banks . . . and deep water.

"Food—insects—are produced mostly in riffles where there is plenty of oxygen. Trout feed in and below these riffles.

"Find *all three* requirements in one place and you've found the "prime lies" in the river."

Where is the best place to cast a fly?

"Cast so your fly drifts into the seam where the slick water meets the fast. This "foam line" is where insects on the water are carried by the current and where trout feed."

Where are the best places for a beginner to fish?

"Beginners will do better in faster, 'broken' water. Fish don't have time to study the fly or its presentation, and the broken water hides the fisherman from fish.

Slick and glassy water holds some big trout, but is difficult to fish because fish have time to study what they eat and they can see and hear an inexperienced fisherman."

When is the best time to fish the river?

A general rule is to fish when it's the most comfortable for you. When it's too cold, insects and fish are not active, so early and late in the day is not good fishing early or late in the season. When it's too hot, say in the middle of the day in the summer, insects and fish are not active, so early and late in the day are the best times to fish. Of course on this river you also have to take into account the rise and fall of the water level. *(See Chapter 8.)*

How big are the browns in this river?

"Twenty-inch fish are quite common, but I've seen brown trout as long as my leg—30-inch fish."

What length fly rod do you recommend for fishing the West Canada?

"Because this is a big river with plenty of room to cast , a 9-foot, 5-weight rod is best. However, the best all-around rod would be an 8 1/2-foot , 5-weight.
A 5-weight, weight forward, floating flyline with a 9-foot, 5x leader will handle most popular West Canada flies."

Randy's favorite fly is the Golden Drake (that figures), but he believes in matching the hatch whenever possible, especially in runs and pools where brown trout have time to study the food that's in the river. When I asked him to select the 10 best flies for the West Canada, he provided the list and charts I've used in this book. Most of these were the same flies John Bianco recommended, some of them were fished by Jack McDiarmid more than 70 years ago, and a few are flies that have recently appeared on the river.

While Jack, John and Randy are very different individuals they have much in common. They each spent many years learning to take West Canada fish on a fly; they shared their knowledge and skills with

West Canada fly fishermen dream about the hatches and trout at Blue Barn Bend.

hundreds, perhaps thousands, of others; they never stopped learning and teaching, and they fell in love with West Canada Creek. One more thing. Their ultimate challenge was to "hunt" down a big West Canada brown trout, catch it on a fly of their own creation, and return it to fight another day.

10 BEST WEST CANADA FLY PATTERNS

MAYFLIES

1—Light Cahill (#12 & #14)—hatches for about 5 weeks on the West Canada, but this pattern can be used to imitate a large variety of light-colored Mayflies like the Cream Variant and White Fly.

2—Golden Drake (#12–2XL)—very common on the West Canada. Hatches for almost two months in mid to late summer when many other streams are "shut down". Trout often take it with a very explosive rise.

3—Blue-winged Olive (#14–#20) hatch almost all season long and can be found the length of the river (below Trenton Falls). Also hatch

Mayfly Hatches

WEST CANADA CREEK

FLY / INSECT	HOOK SIZE	TIME	APRIL	MAY	JUNE	JULY	AUGUST	SEPT
Quill Gordon	#14	8 a.m.–Noon	▮					
Hendrickson/Red Quill	#14	8 a.m.–dark			▮			
Gray Fox	#12–14	3 p.m.–dark			▮			
Light Cahill	#14	3 p.m.–dark			▮			
Pale Evening Dun	#16	6 p.m.–dark			▮			
Dun Variant	#12	8–11 a.m.			▮			▮
March Brown	#10–12	4 p.m.–dark			▮			
Cream Variant	#14	7 p.m.–dark				▮		
Green Drake	#10–12	4 p.m.–dark			▮			
Golden Drake	#12	7 p.m.–dark				▮	▮	
Blue Quill	#18	varies		▮				
Blue-winged Olive	#18	7 a.m.–dark						▮
White Fly	#14	6 p.m.–dark						▮

Sporadic — *Activity*

heavily in the fall, creating great fishing in October and November. *Randy Kulig uses the Sparkle Dun tie for the Mayflies listed above. Fishes them as a dryfly on the drift and then tugs them under to fish as a wet fly on the retrieve. He calls them "damp flies".*

4—Gold-Ribbed Hare's Ear Nymph (#10–#18)—the "American Express" of trout flies—don't leave home without them. Represents nothing in particular but everything in general. Can imitate mayflies, caddis flies and stoneflies.

5—Prince Nymph- (#8–#14)—represents the numerous Dun Variant nymphs in the West Canada.

CADDIS FLIES

6—"X" Caddis Dry Fly (#14 & #16)—tan, gray and gray wing with green body. Fish with some twitches and hops to imitate the actions of real caddis flies.

7—West Canada Cinnamon Caddis Dry (#10 & #12)—the big Cinnamons don't hatch everywhere on the West Canada, but if some of these big flies are on the water they bring up the biggest fish in the area.

8—West Canada Caddis Emerger (#14 & #16)—works day in and day out. Tied in gray, tan and green to imitate the most common caddis flies. Fish "dead drift", then let the currrent pull it up. That's when fish usually smash it.
(Created by Randy and Carol Kulig)

9—Caddis Pupa (#14 & #16)—tan, gray, sometimes green. Trout jump out of the water when they're feeding on caddis pupa.

10—Disco Caddis Pupa (#14 & #16)—a "sparkley" little pupa that works especially well on the West Canada. Can be tied as a *bead head* for deeper presentation.

Chapter 9
FLOAT-FISHING

The best way to enjoy away-from-the-road fishing on the West Canada is to float the river. While most float-fishermen prefer canoes, some anglers use tubes, kayaks and a variety of small boats. At least one fishing guide floats a section of the river with a drift boat.

Whatever the craft, the idea is to drift along with the current, casting to fish-havens along the way, and stopping from time to time to fish areas that most shore and wading fishermen never see.

I've canoe-fished rivers and streams throughout New York State for more than 30 years. Without a doubt the West Canada below Trenton Falls is the best canoe-fishing stream in the state. In addition to the many opportunities to take fish, there are long stretches of easy-water to canoe ..... and power dam releases almost always guarantee plenty of water even during the summer months.

The longest continuous run of easy-water (no bad rapids, dams or falls) is from Trenton Falls to the Fishermen's Parking Area just downstream from the village of Poland. (Don't be fooled by the calm water here; just around the bend are "expert canoeist" rapids during high water periods.)

Another good stretch of canoe-fishing water is from Newport to Middleville. There is plenty of fast water in this area, but unless the water is low, it's easy to canoe. If the water is low, plan to walk the canoe through some areas. You can launch just below the bridge and power plant at Newport and take out on the west side of the river just upstream from Middleville.

While there are short stretches of river that can be canoe-fished below Middleville, most of this part of the river is kayak water; too dangerous to fish from a canoe.

There are a number of bridges and roadside parking areas along the river, so it's easy to plan a trip for as little as an hour or up to a full day. The first 2.5 miles are Special Trout Waters (See Chapter 3). Below the outlet of Cincinnati Creek, bait as well as lures are permitted.

The river can be canoe-fished even during low-water periods because water is released from upstream power dams around 9 a.m. Canoe-fishermen have a couple of hours to launch during this release and ride it all day. This rising water travels about 5 mph and reaches the village of Poland around noon. Many canoeists make the mistake of thinking the water is high everywhere on the stream at the same time. I've heard them complaining about bottoming out in their canoes because they launched before or after the water-release passed through their section of the stream.

If you wade this stream or beach your canoe before the water rises, be prepared. You can get into big trouble if you're in mid-stream or your canoe isn't tied up.

In addition to fishing gear, paddles and such, you'll need life preservers, preferably life vests, a cooler for drinks and snacks, hip boots when the water's cold and sneakers if it's warm.

Part of the joy of canoe-fishing is seeing wildlife, and the West Canada attracts more than its share. There are respectable populations of merganser and mallard ducks, Canada geese, great blue heron, bittern and osprey that feed on or near the river. Other wildlife that you are likely to see are wood ducks, owls, crows, kingfisher, muskrat, whitetail deer, squirrels and a variety of songbirds.

There are a number of restaurant/diners in the area. I usually stop for an ice cream at the one near the parking/picnic area just downstream from where Routes 8 and 28 meet. (A good place to end or start a short trip) It's called the Blue Anchor, not to be confused with the Blue Rose Restaurant which is also on Route 28, a mile south of Poland ...... and a good place to have dinner after you finish your trip.

There are cabins next to the Blue Anchor Restaurant, and canoe rentals and campgrounds at West Canada Creek Campsites. The West Canada Sport Shop in Middleville also rents canoes, and just south of Middleville on Route 28 is a KOA campground and cabins.

Incidentally, the fishing guide who runs a drift boat can be contacted through the Golden Drake Fly Shop, also in Middleville on Route 28.

WEST CANADA CREEK
INFORMATION AND ACCOMMODATIONS

FISHING TACKLE AND GUIDE SERVICES
West Canada Creek Sport Shop, Rte 28, Middleville—315-891-3804
Golden Drake Fly Shop, Rte 28 Middleville—315-891-3591

CAMPSITES & CABINS
West Canada Creek Campsites, Rte 8 / 28, Deerfield/ Poland—315-826-7390
KOA Campgrounds, Rte 28 Middleville—315-891-7355
Blue Anchor Cabins, Rte 28, Deerfield/Poland—315-826-3444

MOTELS
There are no motels on the river, however, there are many in Herkimer and Utica.
Herkimer County Chamber of Commerce—315-866-7820
Utica Chamber of Commerce—315-724-3151

RESTAURANTS AND DINERS
Blue Anchor Restaurant, Rte 28, Deerfield—breakfast and lunch
Kuyahoora Inn—Rte 8, Poland—Friday fish fry—a trophy trout on the wall
Irwin House—Rte 28, Poland
Blue Rose Restaurant*—Rte 28, between Poland and Newport—breakfast,
    lunch and dinner
West Side Saloon and Steak House—Rte 28, Newport—lunch, dinner—
    view of river
Newport Cafe—Rte 28, Newport—breakfast and lunch
Main Street Ristorante*—Rte 28, Newport—breakfast (weekends), lunch,
    dinner
Reilly's Yankee General—Rte 28 between Newport and Middleville—lunch,
    dinner—view of river.
French's Restaurant—Rte 28, Middleville—lunch, dinner
Bev's Diner—Rte 28, Middleville—breakfast, lunch
Crystal Chandelier Restaurant*—Rte 28 Middleville—lunch, dinner

* *Personal favorites*

OTHER ATTRACTIONS
Herkimer Diamond Mines, Rte 28, Middleville—315-891-7355
Ace of Diamond Mines, Rte 28, Middleville—315-891-3855
Herkimer County Historical Society Museums, Main St, Herkimer—
    315-866-6413
Heidelberg Bakery (old world breads)—Rte 28, Herkimer

ABOUT THE AUTHOR

M. Paul Keesler started fishing West Canada Creek in the early 60s, and began his long career as an outdoor writer in 1966 with a magazine article about fishing and canoeing West Canada Creek. For several years he wrote the *About Fish and Game* column for the *Utica Observer Dispatch*, and for a couple of years hosted the *Mid York Sportsman Show* on WUTR TV.

In 1972 he founded the *Mid York Sportsman* magazine which became the *New York Sportsman* in 1975. In 1992 he retired as Editor of the magazine to devote more time to researching and writing books about outdoors New York State. Three years later he published ***Canoe-Fishing New York Rivers and Streams.***

Keesler continues to write feature articles for the *New York Sportsman*. His current book-project is ***Kuyahoora—Discovering West Canada Valley.***

He is also the author of the book ***One Quarter Mile To Go—The Bicentennial Re-creation Of The March of the Tryon County Militia and The Battle of Oriskany*** (1978), the co-author of ***New York Sportsman It's Fun To Eat Cookbook (1985)*** and of course the author of ***Guide to Fishing West Canada Creek and Its Tributaries***

He lives with his wife Gert and and their two golden retrievers on the banks of West Canada Creek.

THE BIG BOOK IN 1998

KUYAHOORA
DISCOVERING WEST CANADA VALLEY

In 1994 I started to gather information for a book that would tell the West Canada Valley story. What started as a quest for information became a path to discovery. When I read about the settlers who first came to this region; how many of them walked from Little Falls to Fairfield and on to Norway and Russia, I walked that same path to see how long it took, how difficult it was and what it looked like.

When I read about the gristmills and sawmills that harnessed the water in the tributary streams, I walked these streams to see the waterfalls, the remnants of old mills and the wildlife and wildflowers. I carried a notebook, a camera and a fishing rod.

When I read about the communities that grew around these mills and along the river, I walked through every one of them again and again. When I read about the headwaters where French Louie had his wilderness retreat, I backpacked into the West Canada Lakes Wilderness Area to see what it was like to fish and hunt in this remote region. When I read about Trume Haskell's wilderness camp, I stayed the night, hunted Polack Mountain and read 50 years of camp guest books.

I studied old maps and new maps to better understand the lay of the land and the flow of the water. What I couldn't see afoot, on snowshoes or skis, or from a canoe or car, I saw and photographed from a helicopter.

I fished and canoed the river and creeks, hunted the woods for game and wildflowers, hiked, skied and snowshoed the trails, climbed up the highest hills, climbed down the deepest gorges, felt the power of the mightiest waterfalls and marvelled at the beauty of West Canada Valley from every angle.

I interviewed people who live, work and play here: farmers, restaurant owners, diamond mine owners, campground owners, educators, biologists, geologists, power plant operators, public servants, politicians, fishermen, hunters, canoeists and kayakers. The list goes on and on, and I'm not done yet.

I will be done in the fall of 1998. That's when I plan to publish what I have come to call *"The Big Book"*. It will feature more information, photographs and maps on West Canada Valley than has ever been published in a single volume. Much of it will be in color. All of it will be chock full of information about this fascinating region of New York State.

Kuyahoora—Discovering West Canada Valley will be big, colorful and ⌐ ˋensive to publish. If you're interested in receiving a pre-publication discount ˋ, write to WC Valley Book, Special Discount, Box A, Prospect, NY 13435. ˋ expires on September 23, 1998.

M. Paul Keesler